The Tabloid Press

A teacher's guide

Jo Wilcock

Auteur

Jo Wilcock

Jo Wilcock is the Director of Southern Film Education and author of the **Documentaries** publications for Auteur. She taught Media Studies in schools and colleges for six years and is currently an Examiner for AQA Media Studies GCSE and VCE Media: Communication and Productions.

Dedication

For G - here's to 4.4.02, for keeps.
For B - keep smiling, darls.
For N - with memories of Peter Pogle!

Rupert Murdoch still courtesy of *The Guardian*

First Published 2001

by Auteur

The Old Surgery, 9 Pulford Road, Leighton Buzzard, Bedfordshire, LU7 1AB

ISBN 1 903663 08 3

Auteur on the internet: http://www.auteur.co.uk

Designed and typeset by Loaf, PO Box 737, Cottenham, Cambridge, CB4 8BA

Printed by The Direct Printing Company, 4-6 Staveley Way, Brixworth, Northants, NN6 9TX

Contents

'Tidings - the report or account of recent events or occurrences, brought to or coming to one as new information; new occurrences as a subject of report or talk.'
Oxford English Dictionary

'Up 'til now it has been thought that the growth of the Christian myths during the Roman Empire was possible only because printing was not yet invented. Precisely the contrary. The daily press and telegraph, which in a moment spread intentions over the whole earth, fabricate more myths ... in one day than could have formerly been done in a century.'
Karl Marx 1871, writing on atrocity stories which appeared in the British press during the Paris Commune

'The word "newspaper" shall mean any paper containing public news, intelligence, or occurences, or any remarks or observations therein printed for sale and published in England or Ireland periodically, or in parts or numbers at intervals not exceeding twenty-six days between the publication of any two such papers, parts or numbers. Also any paper printed in order to be dispersed, and made public, weekly or oftener, or at intervals not exceeding twenty-six days, containing only or principally advertisements.'
The Newspaper Libel and Registration Act 1881, Section 1

'... the expression "newspaper" means any paper containing public news or observations thereon, or consisting wholly or mainly of advertisements, which is printed for sale and is published in the United Kingdom either periodically or in parts or numbers at intervals not exceeding thirty-six days.'
Defamation Act 1952, Section 7(5)

'Newspapers exist to be read ... they are as good or as bad as their public allow, for the greatest newspaper in the world has no future if it cannot get and hold a public.'
Francis Williams, 1959

'News is like the weather except someone makes it up.'
the character of Mickey Knox in the feature film *Natural Born Killers,* 1995

Introduction

The news is arguably the greatest shaping force that the mass media can wield on the general public, in that we as an audience generally accept and form our own opinions based on what we read. Newspapers are cultural artefacts; they differ across countries and cultures and are consequently ideologically loaded, revealing much about the country in which they are published and how key groups within that society are represented by the media. Newspapers are ephemeral; they are written for people to read on a daily basis. The reading of daily newspapers is a kind of ritual for many people, having a place in their daily routine. It affirms that the world 'out there' exists and they have a place in it. In Britain, we read more newspapers than any other European country and our best selling newspaper is *The Sun*, a tabloid. (It is also the best selling English language newspaper in the world.)

This **Teacher's Guide** and the accompanying **Classroom Resources** have been written and compiled for teachers and students of **GCSE** and **AS/A2** Media Studies. They should be particularly useful for those following the following syllabuses: **AQA GCSE** (with special reference to the Summer 2002 exam); **OCR GCSE** Media Studies Paper 1 (Unseen Extracts/National Newspapers, Languages & Categories, Media Producers & Audiences, Media Messages & Values); **NEAB A** level Media Paper 1 (Key Concepts) and Paper 2 (Production and Manufacture of News); and **OCR AS & A2** Media Studies.

Tabloid – 'Proprietary name for a compressed dose of a drug; a popular newspaper; a cheap, sensational newspaper.' **Concise English Dictionary**

What is a Newspaper?

What then is a newspaper? Is it, as the name suggests, a paper that contains news? Or does it contain other elements? How much of the content can actually be defined as 'news'? What is understood by the term 'news'?

National newspapers in Britain can be described as follows:

1. National newspapers are a much stronger medium in Britain than in most Western countries.
2. They are supported by a network of paid-for regional newspapers, mainly evening and weekly titles, and a growing number of free distribution papers.
3. There are 14 national daily papers selling a total of 13.1 million+ copies a day.
4. Fifty-five per cent of the adult population of Great Britain read at least one national daily.
5. There are 11 national Sunday papers selling over 15.1 million copies each week.
6. Sixty per cent of the adult population of Great Britain read at least one national Sunday.
7. There are 18 regional morning newspapers; 72 regional evening newspapers; 7 regional Sunday newspapers and 477 local weekly newspapers.

(Sources: ABC Jul - Dec 1996; NRS Jul - Dec 1996; AA 2001)

In order to come to some sort of understanding of what a newspaper is (in contemporary terms) it is useful to analyse the contents of both a broadsheet and a tabloid to see if any conclusions can be drawn.

Below is a comparative analysis of the content of a tabloid – *The Sun* - and a broadsheet – *The Guardian* - both published on the same day, Monday, 16 July 2001.

Newspaper (price)	*The Sun* (30p)	*The Guardian* (50p)
No. of pages in total	48	146 (22pg main paper; 24pg G2 supplement; 52pg media supplement; 32pg sport supplement; 16pg office supplement)
Pages of domestic news	8 (17%)	10 (7%)
Pages of international news	2 (4%)	6 (4%)
Pages of advertising	15 (31%)	72 (49%)
Pages of sport	10 (21%)	31 (21%)
Pages of entertainment	13 (27%)	27*(19%)

* For the purposes of this exercise I have included the written content of the media supplements in the entertainment category, as opposed to domestic news, as the articles reflect the entertainments industry (i.e. the media).

The following points should be considered:

- *The Guardian* has more pages then *The Sun* and a total of four supplements, whereas *The Sun* has none.
- *The Guardian* is almost half (49 per cent) advertisements (including job adverts) and *The Sun's* advertisements are almost a third of its total page number (31 per cent).
- This high level of advertising would account for *The Guardian's* total page number.
- Domestic news predominates over international news for both, with *The Guardian* carrying a greater proportion than *The Sun*.
- *The Sun* has a greater emphasis on entertainment (27 per cent) and sport (21 per cent) then *The Guardian*, whose respective figures are 19 per cent and 21 per cent.
- *The Guardian* provides greater value for money for the cover price by virtue of its greater page limit (remembering that one page of a broadsheet is twice the size of a tabloid) but not for the amount of pages actually dedicated to news, since 49 per cent is advertisements.
- The dedicated supplements in *The Guardian* indicate the newspaper's belief in the importance of those subjects to their readers.

It can certainly be argued that readers, in particular those who read tabloids, do not read their newspaper solely for their news content. 'News' as defined by the content of newspapers is also stories about the Royal family, celebrities and sporting events. Tabloids, in their pursuit of giving their readers what they want, do not elevate stories about politics, war or famine above an item on the latest exploits of topless model Jordan or the on – off relationship of Puff Daddy and Jennifer Lopez; items on popular culture are signalled as being equally valid since they are of interest to their readers. On the whole tabloids reinforce the dominant ideology, they do not seek to question or challenge but adopt a set of 'best-fit' values.

The conventions of a tabloid

Names: *The Sun; The Express; The Mirror; Daily Mail; News of the World; Daily Star; The Express on Sunday; Mail on Sunday; Sunday Mirror; The People.*

Size: 14.5" x 23".

Ratio of images to words: tend to have a higher percentage of photos, illustrations and other visuals than broadsheets.

Style/tone: often sensationalist/exaggerated with a keen use of alliteration and puns.

Content: tend to focus on entertainment/popular culture items with politics and sport represented as well.

Language: easy to understand, colloquial/everyday, simple syntax, short paragraphs.

Target audience: read largely by the working and lower-middle classes.

NB Tabloids can be further sub-divided as follows:
Middle Market – e.g. *Daily Mail* and *The Express* – medium circulation with a mid-market readership and a balance of news and feature material.
Popular – e.g. *The Sun, The Mirror, Daily Star* – low cover price, high circulation, high picture, feature and gossip content.

Journalism

'The collection, preparation and distribution of news and related commentary and feature materials through such media as pamphlets, newsletters, newspapers, magazines, radio, motion pictures, television and books.'
(Encyclopaedia Britannica)

The word 'journalism' was originally used to refer to print-based reports of current affairs, but with the advent of television, radio and other forms of electronic communication, the term is more of a catch-all.

Journalists

'People come to us from other papers who have great reputations and last one week; because we demand a very high standard, very fast, very accurate, very exclusive ... I still think that at The Sun *we've got the highest standard of journalism in Fleet Street. ...We are the best and to stay that way you've got to put in the hours.'*
(Senior journalist for *The Sun*, quoted in Tunstall, 1996)

Journalists are the eyes and ears of any public and in a democratic society they are at liberty to investigate and report matters of public concern.

Freelance journalists (that is, those not on the permanent staff of a paper) can and are used on any publication and, according to Tunstall (1996), up to 25 per cent of journalists working at any one time can be freelance. The advantages are that it allows for greater flexibility – newspapers can hire journalists according to their strengths and track record, and it is cost effective – because of the journalist's freelance status the newspaper saves money as they are not responsible for that person's tax, National Insurance contributions, pension contributions or holiday pay. Certain elements of a tabloid tend to be drawn from outside contributors, such as the TV schedule, the crossword section and astrology.

> *'When it comes to freelancers, then [they] will generally come to us first because at the News of the World we will pay you better money than people like The Mirror ... here you're offered £100 for a tip, but at the Daily Mail we only paid £50 for a page lead.'*
> **(Senior journalist for the *News of the World*, quoted in Tunstall, 1996)**

A Brief History of Journalism

The earliest recorded journalistic product was a Roman news-sheet – *Acta Diurna* – which was published in 59BC and covered significant social and political news. The news-sheets were hung on walls in prominent places to ensure as many people as possible read them, however it important to remember that few people at that time were literate so their 'reach' was not very widespread.

In China, a court circular or pao, was circulated amongst government officials during the Tang dynasty and continued to be in use until the Ch'ing dynasty in 1911. However, the first newspaper to be published with any regularity was produced in Antwerp and other German cities in 1609, with England following suit 23 May 1622 with the *Weekly Newes* (published by Nicholas Bourne and Thomas Archer); this was England's first news book to carry the date of the publication on the title page. In 1641 the Star Chamber was abolished and reporting on Parliament commenced in the Diurnall Occurrences in Parliament. There was a distinct rivalry between Royalist (*Mercurius Aulicus*) and Parliamentarian (*Mercurius Britannicus*) newspapers at the time and in 1655 Cromwell ordered all newspapers except official publications (i.e. *Mercurius Britannicus*) to be banned. Control over the press was somewhat erratic. In 1662, after the Restoration, the Printing Act heralded more rigorous press control and the collapse of the Licensing Act in 1679 saw a wave of unlicensed newspapers that ended in Parliament's decision against renewal of the Act in 1695, paving the way for a free press.

With the increase in available printing materials and with greater access to news sources many of the different types of newspaper that we take for granted today were founded and produced for their own specific audience. It is estimated that the first provincial newspaper – the *Norwich Post* - was published on 6 September 1701. The first weekly newspaper, *The Daily Courant* was published on 11 March 1702 (until 1735) and the first evening newspaper – *The Evening Post* – was published in 1706 (the first daily evening newspaper was printed on 3 May 1788 – *The Star* and *Evening Advertiser*). Interestingly, the first Copyright Act was passed in 1709 and between 1738 and 1763 any reporting on Parliament was prohibited; the press later won the right to report on Parliamentary proceedings in 1771.

Origins of the tabloids today

Title	Established	Comments
News of the World founded by John Browne Bell	1 October 1843	• It initially sold for 3d and newsagents refused to sell it for that price. • Bought by Rupert Murdoch in 1969. • Launched the magazine supplement 'Sunday' on 6 September 1981.
Daily Mail launched by the Alfred Harmsworth (later Lord Northcliffe)	4 May 1896	• In 1897 the *Mail* printed largest news illustration by any British newspaper at that time to accompany the Diamond Jubilee procession.

Daily Mail cont...		• Published the first British comic strip – 'Teddy Tail' in 1915.
		• Publishes the first photograph to be transmitted by beam radio (from Melbourne to London) 18 October 1934.
		• *News Chronicle* (formed by the merger of the *Daily News* and the *Daily Chronicle*) merged with the *Daily Mail* in 1960.
		• Sir David English (who transformed the paper's fortunes) died 10 June 1998.
Daily Express launched by Pearson	24 April 1900	• First national daily to put news on the front page.
		• Bought by Max Aitken (later Lord Beaverbrook) in 1916.
		• Controversially sold by Labour peer Lord Hollick to pornographic magazine owner Richard Desmond in 2001.
Daily Mirror launched by Alfred Harmsworth	2 November 1903	• The first daily illustrated exclusively with photo graphs.
		• Robert Maxwell bought The Mirror Group in 1984.
Daily Sketch launched	2 March 1909	• Merged with the *Daily Mail* in 1971.

Daily Herald launched	25 January 1911	• First newspaper to sell two million copies. • The paper was renamed *The Sun* 15 September 1964. • *The Sun* was re-launched as a tabloid by Rupert Murdoch 17 November 1969.
Sunday Express launched	29 December 1918	• Published the first crossword in a British newspaper 1924. • Launched the magazine supplement 3 May 1931.
The Daily Star launched	2 November 1978	• Was printed simultaneously by facsimile in London and Manchester in 1980.
Mail on Sunday launched	2 May 1982	• Was the first photo-composed national newspaper in Britain.
Today launched by Eddie Shah	4 March 1986	• First national colour news paper. • Bought by Rupert Murdoch 1987. • Ceased publication 17 November 1995 (the first national to close since *The Daily Sketch*).
Sunday Sport launched	14 September 1986	
News on Sunday launched	26 April 1987	• Ceased publication November 1987

Reuters

Early newspapers were censored by the government (who also levied taxes on them). However, by the eighteenth century journalists began to enjoy more freedom as their role as reporters of current affairs was recognised as a significant one. The demand for and circulation of newspapers grew as society became more literate and printing became first steam and then electronically driven. In the eighteenth century, alongside current affairs there was a desire for stories on the more popular actors, the theatre, war and any royal gossip. Adverts also focused on the popular interests of the time: theatre, crime, stolen property and medicine. Compared to newspapers of today they were very rudimentary. There were no photographs (it took until the 1920s for black and white photos to be printed and the late 1960s for colour images). As the print was small, people had to read them either during the day or by candlelight as there was no electricity. People's consumption patterns therefore differed to what they are today.

Ultimately, with newspaper circulation reaching the millions and the people's desire for news from home and abroad growing, news agencies were created whose sole purpose was to gather international news that they could then sell on to international newspapers. The development of wired communication facilities – at first the telegraph, the radio, satellite and now the Internet - has enabled a faster, more efficient and more cost-effective system for news gathering and distribution and increased the competition between the different newspapers to get the best coverage.

In the twenty-first century journalism is a recognised profession that operates according to a strict code of conduct. The reasons for this development are fourfold:

- the increasing organisation of journalists;
- better training courses;
- improved availability of information at journalist's disposal;
- an increasing sense of social responsibility by journalists.

Newspapers continue to shape opinions in the 'global village' of the twenty-first century. Consequently, international preoccupations are of concern to the individual and individual tragedies are played out on the international stage. With the now commonly held view that we, the public, are entitled to know enough about what is going on in the world to participate successfully in public life, the journalist is deemed to have a duty to inform us.

The Tabloid Press Today

Post-war Britain has seen the press tending towards more traditional stories which are either dramatic or sensational (preferably both). The increased prominence of the tabloids – they are the best selling newspapers in the UK – has seen a return to politics, sport, crime, sex and showbiz as the staple diet for most tabloid readers, under the banner of 'human interest'.

According to Tunstall (1996), tabloids often lead the way and set the news agenda that other newspapers follow according to their own in-house style:

• the 'human interest' agenda is led by a downmarket tabloid 'exclusive';
• this is followed by a mid-market dailies;
• then the more up-market broadsheets on 'what the tabloids say' but with a weightier angle on the story.

There is no doubt, however, that tabloid newspapers outsell their broadsheet competitors on a regular basis; they are the nation's favourites.

An excellent source of information on the history of journalism and mass communication can be found at: www.ibiblio.org /journalism/ jhistory

National Newspaper data for June 2001

	Overall total average net circulation (UK)	Sub-total circulation (UK)	Fullrate sales (UK)	Lesser rate sales (UK)	Pre-paid Non-postal Subscription sales (UK)	Multiple copy sales (UK)	Sub-total circulation (Rep. Ireland)	Full Rate Sales (Rep. Ireland)
National Morning Popular								
The Mirror	**2,194,866**	2,046,659	1,795,956	194,648	———	56,055	86,852	18,187
Daily Record	**596,255**	571,900	555,652	5,164	———	11,084	1,823	1,823
Daily Star	**611,584**	595,961	528,330	67,603	———	28	———	———
The Star – Republic Of Ireland	**98,881**	4,957	4,957	———	———		93,806	93,239
The Sun	**3,452,588**	3,226,652	3,159,290	103,960	———	3,402	105,354	105,354
National Morning Mid Market								
Daily Express	**940,961**	907,838	820,979	39,087	75	47,697	4,041	4,041
The Daily Mail	**2,445,462**	2,352,598	2,285,765	18,578	———	48,255	7,941	7,941
National Sunday Popular								
News of the World	**3,923,421**	3,680,292	3,510,579	165,959	———	3,754	153,552	153,5552
Sunday Mail	**695,248**	669,936	652,681	3,353	———	13,902	3,133	3,133
Sunday Mirror	**1,832,717**	1,722,113	1,430,749	238,641	———	52,723	50,013	10,013
Sunday People	**1,387,808**	1,287,365	1,257,962	88	———	29,315	62,335	62,335
Sunday Sport	**202,540**	202,540	202,540	———	———			
National Sunday Popular								
Sunday Express	**872,869**	836,703	795,280	10,007	114	31,302	4,955	4,955
The Mail on Sunday	**2,356,590**	2,257,198	2,137,083	57,241	———	62,874	18,449	18,449

(Source: www.abc.org)

Regional Press

In addition to the national press, each region has their own discrete local newspapers that contain a mixture of national and local news and information. Following the format of national newspapers the local press enables its readers to have a wider knowledge of their area as well as an insight as to how their area relates to the country as a whole, with the emphasis very much on the region as a community.

The regional spread of newspapers resembles the following:

Type of newspaper	When published	Cost	Total number
Daily and Sunday titles titles	Mornings	Paid	19
	————————	Free	7
	Evenings	Paid	74
	Sundays	Paid	11
	————————	Free	9
Weekly paid titles	Weeklies	Paid	517
Weekly free titles		Free	666
Total			**1,303**

(Source: NRS database as at 27 March 2001)

**Total UK Regional Press ABC Marketing
Performance July – December 1999 – 2000**

Type of newspaper	Jul-Dec 1999	Jul-Dec 2000	% change 99/00
Mornings paid	1,652,014	1,634,746	-1.05
Mornings free	330,786	687,099	+107.72
Evenings	4,018,671	4,082,941	+1.60
Sundays	1,981,806	1,982,357	+0.03
Weeklies	5,614,831	5,582,068	-0.58
Total	**13,598,108**	**13,969,211**	**+2.73**

Based on all titles with ABC figures for each period.

(Source: ABC Market Performance – Circulation and Distribution 2001)

New Values and News Selection

'News is not the newsworthy event itself, but rather the "report" or "account" of an event ... it is a discourse made into a meaningful "story".
(Hartley, 1993)

'[R]esearch on "news values" would suggest that the processes whereby certain stories come to be seen as "news" in the first place are based not on ideological biases, or ... assumptions about how [the audience] will ... understand and interpret information, but also on assumptions about their emotional reactions. The decision to include or reject a particular item, to tell a story in certain sequence, or to select accompanying visuals ... is based on assumptions about what will grab [their] attention or what they will find exciting or moving or even upsetting.'*
(Buckingham, 1996)

*Buckingham's research focused largely on TV news but is arguably still very true of newspapers.

News is about information – the word is derived from a late Middle English word meaning 'tidings, new information about recent events'. Thus, it is reasonable to state that newspapers are a storytelling medium. They present situations or incidents to an audience via factually based stories. News does not occur naturally or spontaneously; it is gathered and written by paid professionals for mass consumption. It is pretty pointless for a journalist to write a news item that will only be of interest to a minority of people. Newspapers, as with any mass media text, are in the business of making money, so the solution to this, particularly with the tabloid press, is to be populist in

Circulation Figures: Daily Papers

Title	Circulation (000s)	Readership (000s)	Cover Price
The Times	791	2016	40p/50p(Sat) 10p (Mon)
The Guardian	397	1234	45p/60p (Sat)
The Daily Telegraph	1084	2658	45p/75p (Sat) 40p (Mon)
The Independent	265	903	40p/50p (Sat)
Financial Times	297	663	70p
Daily Mail	2091	5283	35p/40p (Sat)
The Express	1195	2784	35p/40p (Sat)
The Sun	3981	10,099	28p
The Mirror	2408	6139	30p
Daily Star	671	2132	30p
	13,180	33,911	

(Sources: ABC Jul–Dec 1996; NRS Jul–Dec 1996: prices as of 1996)

your choice of content, a kind of 'give them what they want' approach. It is also worth noting that fewer people have their newspapers delivered direct to their home nowadays and there is a greater tendency to 'paper-hop' with readers not remaining 100 per cent faithful to the same publication; as a result of this volatile buying behaviour competition is extremely fierce, with newspapers employing a range of sales devices to 'lure the reader in' (e.g. cheap flight deals; free cinema tickets; complimentary recipe cards or CDs).

Each newspaper has its own notion of what makes a 'good story' and will present that story according to its own 'in-house' style and ethos. It will have its own style of address according to its readership. For example, *The Sun* uses a lot of puns, cockney/colloquial terminology and raucous overstatement. As a result some might say that a newspaper can never be objective since it is operating within the framework of its in-house style.

Circulation Figures: Sunday Papers

Title	Circulation (000s)	Readership (000s)	Cover Price
The Observer	453	1265	£1
The Sunday Times	1325	3875	£1
The Sunday Telegraph	776	2140	70p
Independent on Sunday	287	966	£1
The Mail on Sunday	2106	6134	85p
The Express on Sunday	1177	3078	75p
News of the World	4506	11,819	55p
Sunday Mirror	2438	7059	55p
The People	2050	5261	55p
	15,118	41,597	

(Sources: ABC Jul–Dec 1996; NRS Jul–Dec 1996: prices as of 1996)

Newspaper Definitions

The following two definitions of 'news' act as a good starting point for any study of newspapers:

1. News is an end product of a complex process – a process which concerned the sorting and selecting of events according to a socially constructed set of events.
(Hall, 1980)

2. News (on television and in the press) is not self-defining, it is not 'found' or 'gathered', but rather it is 'made'. News is a creation of a journalistic process and is therefore a commodity.
(Philo, 1980)

The notion of what makes good news is complex but there is a specific process involved which emphasises the fact that news is constructed or made and that in this transformation process, mediation (pg. 39) takes place. News is not just what happens in the world but what those who present the news regard as 'newsworthy' to

21

us, the consumer. Thus the idea that news undergoes a process of selection is an important one, as is the consideration of the criteria by which the news is selected.

News Selection

In practical terms the criteria by which news is selected in editorial practice is unconscious. However, for the sake of academic study we must dig deeper and take a closer look at what filters or restricts the news that appears in our newspapers. Similarly, we must also unpack the idea that any news report is objective, since as a discourse its relation to the real is far from straightforward despite its claims for neutrality. News is inherently subjective; any form of information which is passed between a string of people, each with their own agendas and beliefs, could never be objective. The changes to the actual event in the news we receive do not end there. When we read an article we bring to that reading our own socialisation and background; our upbringing and our life experiences will effect how we 'receive' the news we read (e.g. the extent to which we sympathise with a particular country or political party; how we feel about the monarchy or capital punishment).

Another factor that affects the news that we read is the source of the story. Anyone who supplies the information which provides the basis for a news report (e.g. a news agency, a member of the public, a witness to a crime) has his or her own agenda. And often part of this agenda is finance – they want to be paid for their story. All newspapers are in competition with one another, they are businesses and are therefore motivated by sales figures. Their readers are a commodity to them and each news item is produced with their notion of audience in mind.

For any news report to appear in the final version of a newspaper it must have been selected for inclusion at least twice: to be reported on in the first place and then to be chosen by the editor for the final content of a newspaper before it goes to print. Thus to appear in a newspaper at all an event is subject to immense scrutiny and the process of news selection is vital, not least because it outlines a newspaper's code or ideology. It is worth noting here that the readership of a newspaper will be unaware of any omissions to the content of the newspaper. They unconsciously accept what they are presented with as a true reflection of what is going on in the world around them; there is a definite level of implicit trust, a kind of passive acceptance, on their part, that the newspaper (and therefore the editor) will give them what they want to read.

In 1997, Durrants – a press cuttings agency* – started to monitor the types of subjects which were covered by the British press. Their findings offered some interesting insights into the topics and personalities that are deemed newsworthy by British newspaper editors. Basing their findings on an analysis of ten national newspapers and six regional newspapers (in Edinburgh, Liverpool, Cardiff, Norwich, Portsmouth and Birmingham) the report revealed that the Labour Party had received ten times as much coverage as the Conservatives. In terms of their daily content, it was discovered that reports on overseas news tended to be negative, especially in the tabloids, and that the coverage of sports was almost double that of the economy. Coverage of science and sports was predominantly more positive than other topics. And, in the list of 'headline grabbers', sport and the economy were the most newsworthy subjects, with politics, crime, the arts, health, education, Europe, transport, sex, royalty and, finally, the weather coming last. The personalities to gain the most press attention were (in order): Diana, the Princess of Wales; Tony Blair; Sarah, Duchess of York; John Major; Michael Atherton; Prince Charles; Tim Henman; the Queen and Richard Branson.

(Source: The Times, 26 February 1997)

*A press cuttings agency works on behalf of a client who wishes to assess how and where their company is reported. To this end the agency reads an enormous number of newspapers and magazines published and then presents their client with a report.

This selection process is, in reality, an unconscious act for the editor of any newspaper, but the criteria by which news items are selected is known as 'news values'. The study of news values is fundamental to any analysis of a newspaper since it relates to why any news item appears in a newspaper in the first instance, as well as how it is

Examples of political affiliation in tabloid newspapers:

The Daily Mail:
Conservative

The Sun and **News of the World:**
Formerly Conservative, now Labour (as of their election victory in 1997)*

The Express:
Historically Conservative, increasingly left-wing

The Daily Star:
Conservative

The Daily Mirror:
Labour

The Sport:
Labour

presented and where it appears in that newspaper. It relates to how a newspaper is constructed. According to the Royal Commission on the Press in Great Britain, to qualify as news an event must be of interest to the public (the 'public' here meaning the audience for each individual paper).

Events are not intrinsically 'newsworthy' – they only become news when they are selected. Clearly there are many events going on in the world at any one time and what we as consumers of newspapers will read can only ever be a reflection of all of those events. Thus, the process of news selection renders our view of the world a partial one. Similarly, each newspaper will select different stories to focus on so your choice of newspaper will directly affect your knowledge of what is going on in the world outside your door in terms of what you know, how much you know and your take on what you know. The political, social and economic position of the newspaper that you read will have an impact on the information you receive. For example a newspaper which affiliates itself with the Labour Party (e.g. *The Mirror*) will present its coverage of an election or a budget very differently to a

---

A comparison of The Sun's *coverage of the 1992 and 1997 general elections makes for an interesting case study on bias since between those dates the paper changed political allegiance from staunch Thatcherite Conservative to New Labour (or as Roy Greenslade, writing for* The Guardian *put it,* The Sun *had become 'Tonier-than-thou' (25 April 1997)).*

What is particularly interesting about this shift in political allegiance for The Sun *is that in making the decision to change the tone of their news items they were also making a much more difficult (and unprecedented) decision to educate its readers into loving the old enemy – the Labour Party. Naturally, seeing an opportunity to attract a whole new sector of potential voters the Labour Party did all it could to help the newspaper with Tony Blair giving 'exclusive' stories on a regular basis.*

One ironic point though is that whilst this news shift was taking place one regular columnist for The Sun, *Norman Tebbit (ex-Conservative Cabinet Minister and Party Chairman) was continuing to support his old party. On the same day in April 1997 that the paper led with an attack on John Major for conceding a vote on the single currency, Tebbit wrote a piece which stated, "Our currency is only safe in the hands of John Major"!*

newspaper which affiliates itself with the Conservative Party (e.g. *The Daily Mail*). Any news report that you read will be pre-judged by a journalist and skewed in some way as a result.

The Importance of Headlines

Language is an extremely powerful tool and journalists are trained to know how they can use language to their best advantage – it can provoke, challenge or undermine; it can excite, incite or appease. Aside from the visuals a newspaper communicates via the medium of language and it is a fundamental method of conveying its ideological stance.

The following are recent examples of headlines:

Tabloid	Date	Headline	Story
The Sun	30 June 2001	'I Should Be So Clucky'	Kylie Minogue's songs help hens lay more eggs
The Star	25 July 2001	'Ear Op Turned Me Into A Stud'	*Big Brother* contestant, Paul Clark, reveals the secret to his success

Headlines are arguably the make or break of an article in that they are more often than not, what draws us to read an article. Indeed, their key function is to convey the gist of a story in very few words and attract the reader to it. If the headline on the front page is strong then their effectiveness is even more important as they are responsible for attracting the potential reader to the paper as a whole and, more importantly, to buy it. Indeed, so important is their seductive function that many tabloid front covers are dominated by one headline and little else (and the amount of space dedicated to that headline is more than the entire article). So, as you can see, they serve a very important function and for this reason it is the job of the editor to actually write the headline; the journalist who wrote the story rarely writes the accompanying headline.

As it is often the headline that grabs the reader's attention the words used need to be short and sufficiently provocative to 'lure the reader in'. It needs to include the facts of the story concisely and can work alone or alongside a visual image. When a headline is juxtaposed alongside it this gives the reader another layer of meaning. The headline is a persuasive piece of text; it is written in such a way that it can persuade people to adopt a certain opinion on the topic it is focusing on and is therefore positioning the reader to take a side, with the underlying assumption being that the reader will take the view of the newspaper itself and that they share this opinion with the other readers. The readers are addressed as a group in a direct manner – i.e. *Sun* readers; *Mirror* readers.

Social and economic factors involved in news selection

Newspaper production is an industry and a business and as such, has a definite place in a country's economic affairs. And, because it is a business, its activities are to some extent determined by a number of factors: the need to make a profit; the way in which the company is organised economically; the state of its relations with other industries; its journalistic practices and production schedule; its relationship with its workforce. All of these elements have a direct impact on not only the paper's reputation, but also what it publishes and how it is presented.

Readership of tabloids according to their social class.

Title	A	B	C1	C2	D	E	15-24	25-34	35-44	45-54	55+	M	F
The Sun	0	5	17	37	26	14	26	19	17	14	24	54	46
Daily Mirror	1	7	19	35	26	13	22	17	16	14	29	55	45
Daily Express	4	19	30	27	14	7	18	14	17	14	37	52	48
Daily Mail	4	22	32	26	9	6	17	15	17	12	21	59	41
Daily Star	1	4	15	37	30	14	29	22	17	12	21	59	41

* All figures are represented as a percentage.
(Source: NRS, 1985)

For example, the majority of newspapers have a financial section even though these pages are of interest to only a minority of their readers; in focusing on people in positions of power and influence such as the Royalty, newspapers are serving the interests of capitalism and in representing trade unions as a disruptive influence (especially to the production of money) newspapers are reinforcing the status quo.

Galtung and Ruge's Theory of News Selection

News values refers to how people who create the news decide what actually 'qualifies' to be included, and as such is a fundamental part of any study of the tabloid press. The following criterion for news selection is a frequently quoted theory in Media Studies and is based on the findings of an academic study by theorists Johann Galtung and Mari Ruge (in Cohen & Young, 1981). They devised a list which they believed were significant contributing factors (with some sub-divided into finer detail) as to how the news is constructed.

Based on the psychology of perception, the theory uses the idea of a metaphor that the world is a set of broad-casting stations which emit a signal continuously which we cannot register all the time; therefore, we have to select what we pay attention to. Galtung and Ruge argued that our perception of what constitutes an event is culturally determined and not a natural occurrence, but they also believed that it related to 'human culture' and therefore should not vary too much globally.

The theory works in the following way:

Selection: The more an event accesses these criteria the more likely it is to be registered as 'news' and reported on in a newspaper. However, the individual factors are not independent of one another – they are inter-related.

Distortion: Once selected, an item will be accentuated based on what made it newsworthy in the first instance.

Replication: This process of selection and distortion will take place at each phase of the process from the actual event itself to the audience reading about it in the newspaper.

Consequently, the more people involved in the chain of events (e.g. journalist, press agency, PR company, reader) the more **selection** and **distortion** occur. The cumulative effect of the different factors is enormous and can ultimately produce an image of an event that is very different from what really happened. In this way it can be likened to a game of Chinese Whispers in that the more people, or 'middlemen', there are involved in the communication of the news, the more likely it is that the end result will be distorted.

The following is a list of Galtung and Ruge's criteria for news selection and an explanation of what each represents:

F1-8 are 'culture free' and based on the 'human culture'.

• **F1 – Frequency**

An event is more likely to be reported if it occurs close to the publication frequency of the medium (i.e. most newspapers are published daily). For example, during a war or similar dramatic event that takes place over a long period of time, reports tend to be published at a climactic point or when there is a problem, rather than on a daily basis.

- **F2 – Threshold:**

This relates to the size or volume of an event in that it is more likely to be reported if it is on a large scale. For example, a car crash involving ten vehicles is more likely to be reported than an incident involving one vehicle. Similarly, the more violent a murder is the greater the scale of the coverage and the bigger the headline.

  - **F2.1 – Absolute intensity**
  - **F2.2 – Intensity increase**

- **F3 – Unambiguity**

A news report that is clear to the reader and is easily interpreted.

- **F4 – Meaningfulness:**
  - **F4.1 – Cultural Proximity**

    News events that occur near to the country in which the newspaper is published are more likely to be covered since we are more likely to be culturally similar. For example, we are more likely to read about events in France than in Albania since France is nearer to us geographically.

  - **F4.2 – Relevance**

    If the content of a news report has implications for us as a country then its lack of geographical proximity will be over-ridden For example, the nuclear explosion in Chernobyl (1986) was reported on in detail since the radioactive clouds were moving westwards towards the UK; and the Gulf War (1991) as so many of the British Armed Forces were directly involved in the conflict.

- **F5 – Consonance:**
  - **F5.1 – Predictability**
    An event that is almost expected to happen or anticipated and is easily received by the consumer as

F3-5 relate to a consumer's ability to make sense of an incident and discern a clear meaning from the information presented to them.

F4 and its two sub-divisions promote the fact that newspapers promote an ethnocentric ideology (i.e. a consensual model of society that defines certain groups within that society to be 'alien').

a result. For example, violent behaviour at football matches abroad by hooligans.

- **F5.2 – Demand**

An event which we want to happen. For example, a wedding of a member of the Royal family or a famous film star.

- **F6 – Unexpectedness:**

  - **F6.1 – Unpredictability**

  An event which occurs without warning. For example, the Paddington rail crash (1999), the Indian Earthquake (2001), or the terrorist attack on the World Trade Centre in New York (2001).

  - **F6.2 – Scarcity**

  An event which rarely occurs. For example the Indian Earthquake (2001), the 'Sophiegate' scandal (2001), Great Train Robber Ronnie Biggs's return to the UK due to ill health (2001).

- **F7 – Continuity (or 'Inheritance')**

Once news has 'hit the headlines' it will continue to be newsworthy for a while. This is particularly true of disasters or stories which touch the public in some way or affect our daily lives. The reason for this may be inertia in the system or the fact that what was unexpected may now be familiar. For example, the imprisonment of 'Moors Murderers', Ian Brady and Myra Hindley (1994), the Oklahoma bombings (1995), the shootings at Dumblane (1996), the death of Princess Diana (1998), the outbreak of Foot and Mouth Disease (2001).

- **F8 – Composition and balance**

The 'newsworthiness' of an event depends on what else is available for selection that day to be included within the newspaper. (NB: this reinforces Hall's theory that the news is socially constructed.)

- **F9 – Reference to elite nations**

  An event which occurs within one of the more powerful/dominant countries in the world (a.k.a. 'superpowers'); this is particularly relevant if the event is politically or economically based. For example, an election in North America or Russia.

- **F10 – Reference to elite persons**

  A report that focuses on a person who is intrinsically important or whom the general public admires or identifies with. For example, the marriage of 'Posh Spice' to David Beckham; the life and death of Princess Diana; the death of newsreader Jill Dando, Prince William starting his university life at St Andrews.

- **F11 – Reference to persons**

  A report which focuses on 'ordinary' people in order to promote a particular reaction from the reader such as empathy, disapproval or identification. Often the people focused on will be personalised to symbolise the issue contained within the report and the pertinent issues of the story will be ignored. For example, the murder of Stephen Lawrence (1993), the arrest of murderers Fred and Rosemary West (1995), the discovery of serial killer Doctor Harold Shipman (1999-2000), the death of Reggie Kray (2000).

- **F12 – Reference to something negative**

  It can be argued that the more negative a story the more likely it is to be reported on (this works on the theory that bad news is more compelling). Similarly negative events occur more frequently than positive ones. For example, disasters such as the murder of the Nepalese Royal family (2001), are more likely to be reported on than triumphs – it is quicker to crash an aeroplane than to build one.

  The extent to which each newspaper can be said to adhere to these factors varies enormously between publications.

F9 - 12 are culturally bound factors (especially the North-Western part of the world) which influence an event's transition from an event to a news item; the more an event satisfies these criteria the more likely it is to be translated into a news report. F9 and F10 demonstrate that the news is elite-centred.

News Sources

Another factor that can be said to have a fundamental impact on the news we are presented with is the actual sources that are monitored as a matter of course by journalists for their 'newsworthiness'. According to Brian Whittaker a number of institutions and events are consistently monitored by the press as a source of news. These can be cited as follows:

Sources which are monitored regularly:

- Parliament
- Councils
- Police (and the Army in Northern Ireland)
- The emergency services
- Courts (including inquests and tribunals)
- Royalty
- 'Diary' events (e.g. Wimbledon; Ascot Races) or conferences (e.g. political parties; trade unions)
- Airports
- Other news media

Organisations which issue statements to the press:

- Government departments
- Local authority departments
- Public services
- Companies
- Trade unions
- Non-commercial organisations such as charities
- Political parties
- Army, Navy, Air Force

Individuals who make statements or seek publicity:

- Prominent people such as film stars, sports stars, pop stars, religious leaders
- Members of the public

As can be seen from the list the source of the news has a clear implication for the content of our newspapers in terms of who is being represented, who is being excluded and how we receive information about these people in terms of the content. Who is written about in newspapers is based on age-old notions of the existence of a social hierarchy and consensus. According to Whittaker, sources used are privileged: they are established as a result of some kind of official authority, social status or commercial success. Unlike the general public, sources monitored are fully equipped to deal with newspapers and journalists – they have systems and resources in place which are responsible for Public Relations, writing press statements, publicity, etc. When members of the public are mentioned their status is accidental and not privileged (e.g. they have witnessed an accident).

Access

By contrast, Hartley (1993) asserted a theory of 'accessed voices'. He believed that the opinions of a privileged body of politicians, civil servants, directors, doctors, members of the Royal family and film stars were actively sought and that the relationship between these 'privileged few' and the press is a reciprocal one, in that the media expect and receive news from these individuals and in return the individuals receive access to the paper and, consequently, publicity. A member of the public would not, ordinarily be expected to call a press conference or indeed be heeded (unless they had been involved in an incident that in itself commanded the attention of the press and then they tend to have guidance/support in their dealings with the press).

The over-riding effect of this is a continued imbalance in representation between the 'privileged' and the 'unprivileged' with the views of the rich and powerful consistently called upon by the press. This skewing of information in favour of the privileged ultimately leads to the press adopting a certain ideological perspective that favours the privileged. The papers continue to voice the opinions of those in power, or who are regarded as powerful, and do so in an authoritative style, adopting the language and attitudes of the elite that reinforce the official ideology of the privileged (e.g. editorials).

The media therefore play a key role on the way that the news is constructed – events are not 'real', they are reconstructed for the readers.

Case study: Noam Chomsky

The American linguist and media philosopher Noam Chomsky asserts that the media is a key player in terms of the way in which those in power communicate to their public, a platform upon which the powerful speak, gain and retain power, particularly when a country is at war. Whilst Chomsky's theory (Herman & Chomsky, 1995) relates primarily to his findings in the American media, what he asserts in terms of how the media manufactures consent amongst a population can quite easily be applied to the British media, and the tabloid press, too.

A bullet point summary of Noam Chomsky's theory of media control is as follows:

- The media plays a vital role in contemporary politics since it forces us to ask ourselves what kind of society we want to live in and what it means to be 'democratic'.

- According to Chomsky there are two different conceptions of democracy:

1. A society in which the public have the means to participate in a meaningful way in the management of their affairs and the means of information are open and free (i.e. this is a dictionary definition).

2. The public must be barred from the management of their own a ffairs and the means of information must be kept narrowly and rigidly controlled. Chomsky believes that this is the prevailing assumption and that it dates back to seventeenth-century England.

- Chomsky refers to the work of Walter Lippmann, a liberal democratic theorist, who argued that what he called 'a revolution in the art of democracy' could be used to 'manufacture consent' (i.e. to bring about public agreement for things that they didn't want by the technique of propaganda). Lippmann felt this to be a good and, indeed, a necessary idea, believing that common interests elude public opinion entirely and could only be managed by a specialised class of responsible men. This theory asserts that only a small elite, an intellectual community, can understand a common interest (which, incidentally, represents a Leninist view).

- Lippmann also put forward a theory of progressive democracy which states that in a properly functioning democracy there are two distinct classes of citizens:

  1. The specialised class - these have an active role in the running of general affairs, they analyse, execute and make decisions, and run the political, economic and ideological systems. These are a small percentage of the population.

  2. The 'bewildered herd' - these are the majority of the population and have a function in a democracy to be 'spectators' of, not participants in, action. Occasionally, they may support one or more of the specialised class; this is called an election. But once that person is elected the herd sink back to their position as spectator.

- This theory is supported by a moral principle that believes that the 'herd' are unable to understand things and therefore need their affairs to be managed; otherwise the 'herd' become unmanageable. Thus their control is achieved via the manufacturing of consent and the media, schools/education and popular culture are divided: one system is directed at the specialised class to indoctrinate the values/interests of private power, the rest is basically there to distract the 'bewildered herd'.

- In a totalitarian/military state the people are ruled by force. In a democracy you lose that capacity and therefore, Chomsky argues, the elite have turned to propaganda to achieve the same end. The USA pioneered the public relations industry in its commitment, 'to control the public mind'; these days it costs billions of dollars a year to do so. For Chomsky, a good illustration of this is how the PR industry was used in the Gulf War. The Americans were bombarded with messages to 'support our troops' but as Chomsky points out, such statements are meaningless since they don't focus on the fundamental issues at stake (in this instance, the threat to the oil supply to the West). This is good propaganda because it diverts our attention.

- According to Chomsky, the media's role, as a corporate monopoly, is to divert attention and marginalise people. By providing sport, sitcoms or violent movies as a distraction and, every so often encouraging the population to chant meaningless slogans, such as 'support our troops', the media encourages a climate of fear and prevents people from thinking too deeply about the political situation around them.

- Prior to the Gulf War it is a lesser-known fact that Saddam Hussein had been a friend and trading partner of George Bush. Now, however, Hussein is perceived as a monster set on conquering the world; it has been drilled into our minds that he will take everything and we have to stop him. How did he get to be so powerful? This is a small third-world country without an industrial base.

- Chomsky asserts that the population tends to be pacifist and sees no reason for killing; therefore, in times of war you have to frighten the people – or 'engineer opinion' – to gain their favour. Again the media provide a useful diversion for this purpose and seek to ensure that people do not unite to articulate their opposition. At the time of the Gulf War, *The Washington Post* advocated the need for the people to be instilled with a respect for 'martial value'. In other words, if you want a violent society that exerts force globally to achieve the ends of its own domestic elite, it's necessary to have a proper appreciation of the martial virtues and not be inhibited by the use of violence.

- Chomsky highlights that in terms of domestic, social and economic problems (i.e. homelessness, unemployment, crime, etc.), America hasn't progressed since the 1950s. Thus, the 'bewildered herd' have to be diverted so that they don't notice; they have to fear an enemy. Every year or two a 'major monster' is created, and conveyed via the media, that the population has to defend themselves against; it used to be the Russians, now it is international terrorists, narco-traffickers, Saddam Hussein, et al. This is combined with news coverage of victories over defenceless third-world armies (e.g. Panama, Grenada), which provides relief in that the population feels saved at the last minute. Whilst this is being reported, Chomsky believes that the population do not pay attention to what is really going on.

- However, a dissident culture has grown significantly, according to Chomsky, since the 1960s; it used to be a narrow movement (mainly students and youths) but now major movements exist such as the environmental, anti-nuclear, feminist and, more recently, anti-globalisation lobby. This has had a civilising effect, despite efforts by the ruling elite to control thought and manufacture consent. Scepticism about power, according to Chomsky, has grown but whether it is sufficient to achieve anything is debatable. Chomsky illustrates this point with the example of the gender gap and attitudes towards military force. In the early 1960s both sexes felt the same way - the use of violence to suppress was just. Now, according to polls, there is a gap of 25 per cent in attitude. The effect of a movement (e.g. feminism) is to enable you not to feel isolated, to reinforce your thoughts, to learn more. Movements are informal, they are a mood that involves interaction amongst people. They alert people to the diversionary tactics of the media.

Bias

Another factor, which affects the way in which consumers construe the news, is 'bias'; although to say that bias exists, fullstop, is a crude way of putting it and as teachers of the media we need to dig somewhat deeper. Drawing on our knowledge of representation is a useful starting point since bias relates to the way in which any news item is presented (or re-presented/presented again) to its audience (e.g. the language used, the way in which the report is structured, what is included and what is excluded from the report).

This ideological role of the media gives substance to Marx's basic proposition that, 'the ruling ideas of any age are the ideas of its ruling classes'.

One could argue that bias is inevitable in any news report since not only do individual journalists have their own opinions but also each newspaper has its own 'in-house' style. Similarly, the news and the institutions that construct the news are all socially, politically and economically situated. Therefore each newspaper will inevitably have its own 'angle' – i.e. a set position within society, an ideological stance.

As readers of a newspaper we assume that what we read is a faithful, accurate account of events that we would otherwise have no experience or involvement with. However, it is important to remember that newspapers are subject to intervention and the decisions of those involved with its production. As with any media form, newspapers are not a transparent window on to the world, and as such are in an extremely powerful position

The importance of 'access'

The content of a newspaper is often determined by who has access to the paper: in other words, which people, companies, pressure groups are able to have their opinions cited or are asked to contribute to a news piece. Clearly anyone can publish a newspaper but to achieve and sustain a mass audience you will need to finance the publication's production and marketing and this is a tall order for most. It is for this reason that minority groups tend not to have a mainstream publication or one which endures (e.g. Spare Rib and Marxism Today both went bankrupt in the 1980s).

in terms of what they choose to present to their readers and how they present it to them. When engaging with a newspaper, the readers make huge assumptions about the content – they assume that what is written about has actually happened and that the facts, as presented to them, are true. What we read about is only a **partial** view of the daily events and occurrences around the world so the selection process is intrinsically biased (see the section on News Selection, pg. 22, for more detail on this issue). Similarly, the language and presentation of a news item will vary enormously between newspapers so there is an implicit bias within the context of how it is reported.

The existence of bias can be explained in a number of ways:

1. Bias exists because of the ideology of democracy (or the idea that this is a free country). As a result of a democracy we have a free press that is at liberty to convey a variety of opinions and seek to report the truth as they see it.

Critique: On the whole people are not trained to be discerning in their reading of tabloids – we are not critical readers and therefore do not see through any slant that a report may contain – we take it as a true and accurate reflection of an event.

2. Since media production as an industry is linked to capitalism, bias is implicit within any media product.

Critique: The only way to alter this would be to seek to change the way in which news is not only produced but also financed.

3. Bias exists as a matter of fact; it is inevitable since everyone has his or her own opinions on any event or situation, therefore, an element of distortion is endemic in every medium.

Critique: An argument such as this allows people to become complacent about the issue of bias.

It is important to note that a newspaper's content, and the bias within that content, will also depend on who owns the press in a particular country. So, in countries with a communist government (e.g. pre-Glasnost USSR) the press is owned by the State with the editors and journalists government employees who are subject to rigorous censorship. In this situation, in addition to reporting the news, the press acts as a platform for the government's views and works to uphold the national ideology. By contrast, in democratic, developed countries (especially Western Europe and the USA) the press enjoys more freedom.

In summary, when considering the tabloid press, 'bias' is a term used to describe the way in the tabloids mis-represent, underplay or ignore a particular point of view. By their very nature certain parts of the newspaper will be biased – the editorials and the opinion columns – but it is important to remember that a newspaper's audience may not be able to detect when they are being manipu-lated because the line between news reporting and opinion moulding may be somewhat indistinct. Similarly, a journalist only has a finite amount of time to cover a particular item and so who they interview, their own views and the amount of space allocated to the piece will have an impact on the way in which it is written by the journalist and received by the reader. Thus, we can conclude that no piece of newspaper journalism can ever be said to be 100 per cent accurate – there are too many layers of intervention and interpretation.

Mediation

The concept of mediation is closely linked to that of bias in that it is implicit within the production of a newspaper and journalistic practice as a whole. Mediation reminds us that all news is manufactured; it refers to the way in which a journalist reconstructs the details of an event after it has been selected as an item to be reported on. This reconstruction of the event will be affected by a number of significant factors such as the journalist's own beliefs and values; how the journalist perceives the event; how experienced the journalist is; how much time is available for the report; what 'angle' the journalist takes on the event, etc. Similarly, after the journalist has submitted his or her report it will undergo another process of mediation when the editor rewrites and reshapes it, and a decision will be made as to where it appears in the newspaper, the accompanying headline and picture (if applicable). The final stage of this process occurs when the reader reads the newspaper; each reader will perceive the report of the event according to his or her own socialisation (i.e. experience and background).

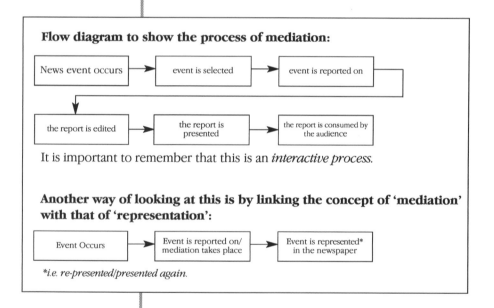

Flow diagram to show the process of mediation:

News event occurs → event is selected → event is reported on

the report is edited → the report is presented → the report is consumed by the audience

It is important to remember that this is an *interactive process.*

Another way of looking at this is by linking the concept of 'mediation' with that of 'representation':

Event Occurs → Event is reported on/ mediation takes place → Event is represented* in the newspaper

i.e. re-presented/presented again.

Spin Doctors

If one is considering the notion of bias within any newspaper it is important to consider the role of political spin doctors and the way in which any political party is represented within the press.

The driving motivation behind any spin doctor is to control journalistic output with the aim of presenting their particular political party in a positive light. As their name suggests they are a kind of political 'mechanic', the person who goes behind the scenes and who knows what issues have to be addressed and what buttons to push to woo and, more importantly, convert voters to their party. As a result of their job they tend to have a very firm grasp of their parties' policies and are highly skilled at sending out simple, crisp messages about the core of their parties' work.

A spin doctor in their role as a 'special advisor' comes under the rules of the Civil Service. When Labour came to power in 1997 Tony Blair decided to employ Alistair Campbell, his Special Adviser, as his Chief Press Secretary. This change to the Service's rules made it possible for a Special Adviser to have the role of Press Secretary, with paragraph 14 (c) of the Special Adviser's contract now reading:

> *'...you are required to conduct yourself in accordance with all the provisions of the Civil Service Code except for those aspects which relate to the impartiality and objectivity of the civil service and civil servants and also which relate to a future administration and potential future ministers.'*
> **(The Guardian, 1997)**

This contract, then, implies that as a Special Adviser the post-holder can make political comments.

If one were to link the work of spin doctors to Noam Chomsky's theory of Media Control one could argue that one of their primary roles is to divert the public's attention from what really matters and work to reinforce the dominant ideology.

Case study: Alistair Campbell – former Chief Press Secretary to the Prime Minister, the Right Honorable Tony Blair MP

Born 1948, the son of a Scottish vet, Campbell attended a Leicestershire comprehensive school before going on to read Modern Languages at Cambridge. His first piece of published writing was some soft porn for *Forum* magazine which he wrote in his twenties* but his foray into serious journalism began when he won a place on the Mirror Group training scheme which led him to gain employment as a writer for the Tavistock Times (it is here that he met his partner Fiona Miller, a former *Express* lobby correspondent who interestingly now works part-time as Cherie Blair's media advisor).

Campbell went on to work his way swiftly through the Mirror Group (apart from a brief spell on the newly-launched *Today* newspaper) and eventually became the political editor of the *Daily Mirror* but quit after a change in management in the early 1990s, to join *Today* once more as their political editor. It was from here that in 1994 he became Tony Blair's Press Secretary – a role which garnered him the nickname of 'the real deputy Prime Minister' – and one which meant that he was responsible for talking to the press on a daily basis, as Blair's official spokesperson. Clearly Campbell's work within the press itself stood him in good stead, for he had a clear understanding as to how the press operate and how to pitch a story to them in order to gain optimum publicity (or alternatively how to gloss over facts which might be detrimental to Labour's image). It was his ability to place a 'spin' on information that has given rise to his extremely high profile image within the press, where indeed the story was often about *him* rather than the information itself. He is renowned for his deft ability to cope with the cut and thrust of arguing with parliamentary lobby journalists.

It was announced (in the press naturally) in April 2001, that Campbell's role as Blair's Press Secretary would come to an end after the June general election 'amid fears of spin overload … and that he has come to symbolise harmful images of Labour spin.' (Nicholas Watt, *The Guardian*, 12 April 2001).

Campbell now works in the less visible but nevertheless, deeply strategic role of Director of Communications at Downing Street (a role which is modelled on the Head of Press at the White House), where he is in charge of co-ordinating the government's fundamental message, rather than briefing journalists on a daily basis as before. This means that he handles Labour's big events, such as liaising with the press for the Budget, as well as any crises that arise.

Some examples of Alistair Campbell's spin-doctoring:

Date	The story	The spin
October 1995	At Blair's second party conference as Labour leader he needed to show that he was a normal guy who was in touch with people	Blair met Kevin Keegan (then Newcastle manager) at a school in Brighton and they played 'head tennis' together
March 1997	John Major calls the general election and Blair needs to attract people's attention	*The Sun* announces that they will be telling their readers to vote Labour
August 1997	The morning after Princess Diana dies Blair is asked for his reaction on his way to church	Blair describes Diana as 'the People's Princess', a Campbell phrase, capturing the nation's mood perfectly
May 1998	British prisoners of war protest about the state visit by Japanese emperor, Akihito	Campbell arranges for *The Sun* to run asigned apology by Akihito for the POW's treatment during WW2
November 2000	The fuel protesters set the government a 60-day deadline to bring forward proposals to help them financially	Chancellor Gordon Brown announces £4.7 billion of fuel-related tax concessions in the Commons

[* The Channel 4 programme *The Mark Thomas Comedy Product* took delight in revealing this fact – see the Web site for an account of this – www.fnord.demon.co.uk/mt/second/campbell.html]

Spin Doctors:
An interesting activity to do is to watch the feature film Wag the Dog *(directed by Barry Levinson, 1998). The film is an excellent, subtle satire, written by David Mamet, about the work of political spin-doctors during an election campaign in the USA. The president has been accused of sexual misconduct by a teenage girl eleven days before the election and a spin doctor, Conrad Bean (played by Robert De Niro), is called in to divert the public's attention away from the scandal until the election is over. Bean hires a Hollywood producer (played by Dustin Hoffman) to 'create' a war for him and to provoke a renewed sense of patriotism in the American public.*

Other political satire films include: The Candidate *(Michael Ritchie, 1972);* Bob Roberts *(Tim Robbins, 1992);* Canadian Bacon *(Michael Moore, 1995).*

Cheque-book Journalism

Everybody loves to gossip. Good gossip is malicious. We live with gossip and we enjoy it.

However, things can get out of hand when tabloids take a piece of gossip too far. In seeking to exploit that gossip they try to achieve additional information more or less by any means necessary (what the late Conservative MP Alan Clarke called a 'blood sport'). Sometimes, in their attempt to acquire that information they 'invest' heavily in a story and enter into a financial arrangement with the source of the information. This commercial (as opposed to journalistic) decision is called cheque-book journalism.

Newspapers have paid people for their story for some time. In the 1920s certain newspapers footed the legal bills of defendants on the promise of an exclusive. More famously in 1963, £23,000 secured Christine Keeler's story of her affair with government minister John Profumo for the *News of the World*. The conventional way to secure information from someone is for a journalist to buy them a drink or pay the person's expenses. Any expert (e.g. a doctor, or a scientist) will be paid a fee if they help to develop a story by offering their own particular knowledge. However, increasingly stories are purchased to secure a newspaper's 'exclusive' rights to that information. The main motivation for this is competitive, a desire to boost sales figures for that particular newspaper since no other publication will carry that story. Thus, the information is limited to that newspaper and to their audience, something which contravenes the idea of a democracy and corrupts the notion of a free press. If a newspaper does buy the exclusive rights to a story then rival publications often try to undermine this by printing 'spoilers' in their publication.

People who do decide to 'sell their story' are often prey to press harassment and give little thought to the long-term consequences of their actions. They will have little influence over how information or their images will be reproduced by the newspaper. Suddenly, their private life (and how the public perceives them) is out of their control with a variety of opinions formed about their words and actions; they are considered public property. It could be argued that their action – the 'deal' that they have struck with a tabloid - serves them right. In being tempted by the prospect of a blank cheque they do not seek legal advice or think carefully about the potential value of their story or whether they have copyright over the information.

One key factor, which we as teachers of Media Studies need to consider when analysing the principle of cheque-book journalism, is the way in which audiences are being positioned. Stories, which are derived from members' of the public stories, are clearly prone to embellishment, or the facts will be skewed in favour of a more 'creative' version of events. However, audiences are not trained to discern fact from fiction and can be somewhat gullible. Also we need to consider what we believe to be acceptable definitions of 'decency', 'taste', 'harassment' and 'distasteful'. So for example, to what lengths do you think a journalist should be allowed to go in the pursuit of a story that is in the 'public interest'? Do you think anyone should be exempt from this method of acquiring of information (e.g. the partner of a person accused of a series of murders; the family of people who have died in a tragic accident)? Interestingly, both of these examples have

Cheque-book journalism is what Tunstall (1996) called the 'buy-up' which he believed followed a sequence:

• Offers are made (often in a sealed envelope).
• A decision made (in conjunction with the person's lawyer, if they are shrewd enough to have one).
• The offer is negotiated (more than one newspaper may be involved).
• An agreement is signed (the naïve may omit to do this)
• The person is moved to a secret place and intensively interviewed (usually by a pair of journalists).
• The story is written in episodic form (to tease it out and optimise income generated by the revelations).
• The 'scoop' is then published (hopefully ahead of any rivals).

actually taken place – Sonia Sutcliffe, the wife of the Yorkshire Ripper, Peter Sutcliffe, was offered money for her story in 1981, as were survivors and relatives of the dead from the Hillsborough disaster in 1989.

Unfortunately, methods used to acquire stories are similar to a game of Chinese Whispers in that there are often many people in the information chain and people can misread, approximate or inflate stories at will as each part of the chain attempts to secure their 'cut'. The result is that the information we receive is more often than not extremely skewed in the newspaper's pursuit of a good story/headline. The tabloids are particularly good at playing this game through a combination of their circulation figures, budgets and their motivating force – a desire for sensation. We are regularly fed a diet of front page scandal and kiss and tell stories as tabloid journalists know that this is what sells – escapism is a commodity with a large price tag on it – and it drives journalists to seek out the information which fuels these stories 'by any means necessary'.

In January 1997 a Commons Committee called for a ban on media payments to witnesses in criminal cases and for a restriction on pre-trial publicity. This came in the wake of some notorious incidences of cheque-book journalism. After the high-profile trial of serial killer Rosemary West in November 1995 (she was convicted of killing ten people), it emerged that nineteen witnesses were believed to have entered into media agreements with newspapers, with some actually receiving money for their story. These payments to witnesses did not affect the outcome of the trial and West was awarded a prison sentence, but the criticism remains that any witness who receives a payment for their version of events may exaggerate, distort or withhold information that would be used as evidence in a court case. And, if they don't do this them-selves then the news article, which is the outcome of their interview with a newspaper, will. Interestingly, other high profile court cases – the Moors murderers, Myra Hindley and Ian Brady; Jeremy Thorpe; the Yorkshire Ripper, Peter Sutcliffe and seventies glam rock star, Gary

Glitter (a.k.a. Paul Gadd) – have all been the target of cheque-book journalism, with witnesses or relatives paid considerable amounts of money for information before, during or immediately after the trial. One problem is described by PCC Chair Lord Wakeham:

'Payments to witnesses, or potential witnesses, by the media, run a real risk of encouraging witnesses to exaggerate their evidence to make it more newsworthy, or to withhold vital evidence from the court and make it available as an exclusive to a newspaper.'
(Lord Wakeham, BBC Newsnight, 14 November 1999)

Witness payments are now subject to much more robust scrutiny and must pass three 'tests' to avoid any accusation of contempt: was payment made in the public interest; did it influence the witnesses evidence; and was it disclosed to the court?

Another infamous case of cheque-book journalism was the news coverage in 1996 of Mandy Allwood's multiple pregnancy. The tabloids were particularly interested in the story as Mandy was expecting eight babies that had been conceived via fertility treatment without the knowledge of her partner, Paul Hudson. The tabloids jumped at the chance of covering this juicy story and the *News of the World* entered into an agreement with Mandy (arranged by PR impresario Max Clifford) whereby she would tell her story exclusively to them. The revelation of the unmarried couple's story and their personal history became public property overnight until her gynaecologist told newspapers that the stress of all the publicity was placing unnecessary strain on the pregnancy and was endangering the unborn babies. Tragically, Mandy lost all of the babies, but having placed herself in the media spotlight already her grief over this loss was also covered by the tabloids. Some might say that she was 'fair game' as she had willingly entered into a contract with a tabloid and 'supped with the devil' so to speak, but others might believe that she had been a victim of the tabloid's seemingly insatiable appetite for a juicy story.

In the autumn of 1995 Central TV undertook an audience survey of 14,000 viewers to seek their opinions on cheque-book journalism: 82 per cent called for a ban.

So why not just ban the practice of cheque-book journalism altogether? According to PressWise, this would be a difficult and not altogether desirable thing to do. Passing the necessary legislation would prove problematic as defining what is in 'the public interest' is nigh on impossible. There is a profound difference between what is in the 'public interest' and that which is just 'of interest to the public'. Similarly the notion of what is 'tasteful' is subjective, so PressWise are keen to see legislation that addresses journalistic malpractice covered under the Contempt of Court Act, rather than a specific ban.

Case study: Max Clifford

Max Clifford is famous, or notorious, in Britain as a publicist whose specialism (or *raison d'être*) is his ability to turn gossip into tabloid cash; the more sensational the story the more cash there is to be made.

His personal profile consists of the following:

• Born 1943.

• Grew up in South Wimbledon, London.

• Left his secondary modern school at 15 years old with no formal qualifications.

• His first job in the media was as a junior reporter on a local newspaper; here he learnt the ropes of the communication business.

• At 19 years old Clifford worked as a publicist for EMI where amongst other work, he promoted a relatively unknown band from Liverpool called The Beatles. At the time the band were struggling for a hit and Clifford was rather loose with the truth, telling one newspaper that the band had sold 50,000 records, as opposed to the 5,000 that was nearer the truth.

• Founded Max Clifford Associates – a Public Relations consultancy, based in New Bond Street, London.

• Max Clifford Associates have represented a range of people from high-profile celebrities such as Mohammed Ali, Frank Sinatra and Marlon Brando to ordinary members of the public who have a story to tell (or sell) the media.

• Ironically, Clifford is these days often more famous than the clients who employ him.

The following are three celebrated examples of Clifford's clientele across the decades:

Client	Year	Story
Freddie Starr	1986	*The Sun* carried the headline 'Freddie Starr Ate My Hamster' after the allegations made by Starr's girlfriend. Starr had responded by posing for a photo with a hamster called Sandwich. Within days Starr's tour had sold out.
Mandy Allwood	1996	Allwood was expecting octuplets and hired Clifford to help her publicise the fact to the press. However, despite achieving media saturation, the deal went sour. Allwood lost all of the babies and later sued Clifford in the High Court in 2001, claiming that he made a secret profit from his work. Allwood won £15,200 in damages from Clifford and another spell in the tabloids as a result. She had initially demanded £16,200 but Clifford had a counter-claim for unpaid commission upheld.
Alison Brown	2000	Brown began a relationship with Gary Glitter when she was 14 years old and sold her story to the *News of the World* for £10,000 while Glitter was awaiting trial for 54 counts of computer pornography charges. She entered into a publishing deal worth a further £25,000 that the tabloid would pay if they used her story should Glitter be convicted. Mrs Brown made a complaint to the police regarding her previous underage sexual relationship with Glitter and he was also charged with eight offences of indecent and sexual assault against her. (She had previously sold her

story to the tabloid in 1987 and again in 1993, proving that her story, in newspaper terms, 'had legs'.) Glitter was acquitted of the sexual indecency charge but later pleaded guilty of 54 counts of possessing child pornography on his laptop and was sentenced to four months in jail.

Once common perception of Clifford is as follows:

'Max Clifford is free to pimp his stories around Fleet Street where editors are seemingly free to ignore the Press Complaints Commission code with impunity and where juries are now taking evidence so tainted ... it really puts in jeopardy our whole system of justice.'
(Lord McNally, Liberal Democrat peer, 23 November 1999)

But how much of the popular negative image of Clifford is itself a construction of the press? Outside of the media spotlight Clifford does a great deal of charity work, donating his fees for after-dinner speaking and TV appearances to good causes and organises tennis coaching for children who live in his neighbourhood. His grown-up daughter has been severely disabled from youth by rheumatoid arthritis and Clifford has used his contacts and celebrity to raise significant funds to help sick children. He has also used his influence to persuade such figures as Muhammad Ali to visit the Children's Cancer Unit at the Royal Marsden Hospital.

Publicity Junkies

'Actors now are more money grabbing. Two TV series stars recently were trying to sell the secrets of their romance to The Sun *for £20,000. We did a tactical wrecking operation ... some of the romance details leaked out, and they got £10,000 for a two parter later in the week.'*
(Senior Journalist for *The Sun*, in Tunstall, 1996)

There are some people in life who are raging self-publicists ... they crave coverage ... they hanker for headlines. These are people who use the media to put themselves in the spotlight as a means to promote themselves. Think Geri Halliwell. Think Liz Hurley. Think Robbie Williams. And ask yourself – just what do Tamara Beckwith and Tara Palmer-Tomkinson actually *do*?

These are the patron saints of the paparazzi and beloved by newspapers on a 'bad news' day. Forget war and famine and foot-and-mouth disease when a celebrity's latest diet, revealing dress or love interest is to be seen and read about. (Why else is *Hello!* – the tabloid celebrity lifestyle magazine – number one in the magazine sales charts?).

People love to read about the lives and loves of the famous but it is the very media that these publicity junkies court that shape the audiences opinion on the 'celebs' themselves. Photos and interviews can be manipulated to suit the needs of the paper. People are represented in ways so that certain traits are highlighted and others ignored with the result that we, as an audience, as receivers of this info-tainment, form quite strong opinions about people we don't know and are unlikely to meet. So, we have an opinion on Geri Halliwell's fluctuating weight; on the 'rock star' behaviour of Liam Gallagher; on 'Nasty' Nick Bateman and on Charles and Camilla's relationship that is shaped for us by the media as a result of how they present 'the facts' as they see it

Fact 1 - The media is undeniably fickle ('who's hot and who's not' fluctuates massively).

Fact 2 - The accuracy of the articles that refer to 'celebs' is often debatable.

Question: Why, then, do people often court the press and, in particular, the tabloids? Stars are a commodity and increase sales, therefore the relationship that a star can establish with a tabloid can be mutually convenient to both parties – the star gains increased publicity (to boost sales of their current book, film or record for example) and shifts newspapers, so everyone wins. Some stars just court the press to keep themselves in the public eye even though they aren't doing much at the time. Alternatively the press keep a star in the public eye because they make for a good story, usually because they have made some huge gaff (e.g. Anthea Turner, Vanessa Feltz, Sarah 'Fergie' Ferguson, Paul 'Gazza' Gasgoine).

Question: Is there such a thing as bad publicity? Judging by the extent of the news coverage in the tabloids when media darling Hugh Grant was caught 'inflagrante delicto' with Divine Brown, and his subsequent incredibly successful film career as a romantic lead, it would seem that publicity is what etches you in people's minds. The fact that we swoon at Grant in films such as *Four Weddings and A Funeral* (1994) and *Bridget Jones's Diary* (2001) means that we, the public, have forgiven him his misdemeanour. If you court the media properly we can forgive anybody anything – ex-Big Breakfast presenter Johnny Vaughan's days in prison for drug offences are smoothed over in favour of his talent as a presenter; Stephen Fry's spell 'inside' is erased from our memory as he is now more commonly known as a dry wit, author and comedy actor.

The Role of Advertising

Advertising is a significant medium in its own right and it is important to remember that advertisements are messages which are constructed to inform or influence the audience that receive (or 'read') them. For this reason it is important that the advertisements are placed where the intended audience (i.e. the target audience) will see them. In Britain, the press and television are the most significant media platforms for advertising, largely because of their huge daily audiences. The advertisers are motivated by the reach of the media.

It is worth remembering that advertising has a fundamental role in the production of all newspapers and in a lot of ways it could be argued that advertising is more important than the news itself, simply because without it there would be no newspapers, or they would certainly be substantially reduced in size and more costly in price. It is advertising which subsidises the newspaper and is a fundamental source of revenue. Because newspapers are a business and are consequently motivated by profit, advertising is paramount. Thus, newspapers operate firmly within the free market system; if they don't make a commercial profit, they fail and they close.

The table overleaf (Fig. 1) indicates the proportions of income that the different types of newspapers receive from advertising and sales.

What conclusions can be drawn from comparing the figures for the national broadsheets and the national popular press? How does this, in turn, compare with the regional press?

The volume of advertising achieved per issue determines the space available for news. Hence, you'll see that there are more adverts in newspapers at the end of the week and over the weekend as there is a market for more news.

Product placement
Many tabloids use product placement to promote themselves, subconsciously lodging the newspaper's title in the minds of their target audiences by placing it strategically within view. Two good examples of this advertising method employed by The Sun *were a large patch on the arm of hunky British tennis star, Greg Rusedski's top whilst he played at Wimbledon (June 2001) and Big Brother 2 evictee, the cheeky cockney lad Bubble, wearing a red* The Sun *baseball cap to the London premiere of* Lara Croft: Tomb Raider *(July 2001).*

Fig. 1 – Proportion of income from advertising and sales

Type of publication	% from advertising	% from sales
National 'quality' press (e.g. *The Telegraph*)	70	30
National popular dailies (e.g. *The Sun*)	40	60
National 'quality' Sundays (e.g. *The Sunday Times*)	70	30
National popular Sundays (e.g. *Mail on Sunday*)	53	47
Regional dailies and Sundays (e.g. *Manchester Evening News*)	71	29
Regional paid-for weeklies	85	15

(Source: Advertising Association 2001)

Below (Fig. 2) are some examples of advertising rates that were set for 1998; the rates are flexible in that they can be subject to negotiation.

Fig. 2

Publication	Advertising rate*
Daily Mail full page (black and white)	£30,492
Daily Mail full page (colour)	£43,974
Daily Telegraph full page (black and white)	£41,125
Daily Telegraph full page (colour)	£49,500

*the rate for each publication will depend on the size of its audience, its age and their social profiles.
(Source: Advertising Association 2001)

Advertisers are interested in a newspaper's sales and circulation figures: the greater the sales and circulation, the greater the reach for the advertiser and therefore the greater the success of the advert and the more likely the advertiser is going to want to invest in the newspaper.

Because the newspaper is reliant on this revenue the editor is more than likely to give the advertisers what they want. It is a mutually beneficial relationship since both mediums – newspapers and advertising – are forms of mass communication and operate within a mass media context.

An understood method of analysing circulation within the industry is the monthly figures provided by the Audit Bureau of Circulation (ABC) who audit the newspapers sales and circulation figures and publishes them alongside a six-monthly rolling average. Sales and circulation figures are ascertained via the following formula:

the number of copies printed
minus
the number of copies unsold (and returned) by the newsagents and wholesalers
equals
the net *sales/circulation* figure.

Nevertheless, whilst these figures are relatively easy to ascertain for newspapers, local or more specialist publications cannot quote such figures which makes any kind of comparative study somewhat unreliable.

It is worth remembering that if a newspaper attracts a large volume of advertising they can afford to lower their cover price. You can prove this by analysing the balance of news to adverts contained in a newspaper that is offering an extremely low cover price in a bid to boost sales. But the advertiser does have additional power: they can have a say about the actual news content since they need it to complement the product that they are trying to promote. So, for example a company that is promoting luxury cars will not want the newspaper to focus on high petrol prices or the problems of British roads. Thus, their desire to sell and the newspaper's need for their revenue have a direct impact on the actual content of the news-papers. How many readers do you think are aware of this profound level of manipulation and ideological 'spin'?

Figures published by The Newspaper Society indicate that in 2000 advertising spend in the regional press was £2,762m, an increase of £279m on 1999, making it the second largest advertising medium behind TV. National newspapers accounted for £2,258m of adspend during the same period. For more information visit: www.newspapersoc.org.uk

There are three main types of advertising within any newspaper – these are outlined in the table below.

Type of advertisement	Description
Classified	Densely packed word-only adverts used by individuals and small companies. The words are written by the people who buy the space (the cost is usually on a penny per word basis) but the paper decides the layout.
Display	These range from a quarter of a page to a double page spread (with the price increasing accordingly). The people who buy the space have control over the content.
Semi-display	This is somewhere between a classified and a display advert with the newspaper having control over the content.

Big Brother 2 – The power of the front page

Big Brother 2 contestant Helen Adams helped boost sales for The Sun *by up to 90,000 per day according to the tabloid. The game show runner-up appeared on the front page of the newspaper nearly every day for the week following the end of the show. According to the tabloid it was her relationship with fellow contestant Paul Clarke which encouraged people to buy the paper for any titbits of gossip on how their relationship was progressing; the newspaper had captured the nation's vicarious interest in the couple's relationship achieving a significant boost to their sales figures at a time of year (i.e. August – the holiday month) which usually meant sales were low.* The Mirror *achieved a similar boost to their sales figures when they featured interviews with the overall winner of Big Brother 2, Brian Dowling; circulation increased by 29,000 in July 2001. In 2000, when* The Sun *signed up Nick Bateman (a.k.a. 'Nasty Nick') sales were boosted by 25–30,000 when he appeared on the front cover and when Melanie Hill was evicted from the house sales increased by 40,000.*

Sales and circulation boosting methods

Newspapers employ a variety of methods to boost circulation figures. Placing bulk copies of the newspaper in hotels, airport lounges and betting shops, for example, will enable newspapers to quote this deposit amongst their bulk circulation statistics.

In May 2001, pornographer Richard Desmond who had recently purchased The Express, The Sunday Express *and* The Star, *had one million copies of* The Express *delivered to homes in the North West and West Country in a distribution deal with the regional group Newsquest (who are owned by Gannett, a US giant). In another bid to boost sales of* The Sunday Express *he gave away complementary copies of the celebrity gossip magazine,* OK! *(which he also owns) and increased the coverage of celebrities in the newspaper itself. In* The Daily Star, *topless model Jordan was used on the front cover of the newspaper on countless occasions. In a neat bit of cross-promotion, Jordan was also featured on* The Star's *television pages every day to promote Television X, Desmond's 'fantasy' channel.*

The Sun *employed two differing methods of boosting sales in 2001. The first was a controversial decision by editor David Yelland in May 2001 to sponsor the return of ailing Great Train Robber, Ronnie Biggs' return to England to certain imprisonment and free NHS treatment. The newspaper carried extensive coverage of the event, claiming that they were bringing the fugitive to justice. However leaks from Wapping suggested that the coup had backfired as the public did not believe that the paper had acted in the public's interest. In addition many of the younger readers were apathetic as they were too young to remember who Biggs was!*

The second sales boost campaign was a joint-promotion between The Sun, *the* News of the World, *and Coca-Cola, in the summer of 2001 which encouraged people to buy the paper and/or the soft drink and collect 'music for you' tokens which could be exchanged for band merchandise, CD's, mini-disc players, instruments or a mixing desk; the idea being that the more tokens you collect – and more papers and drinks bought – the greater the value of gift available to you.*

Newspaper Personnel

The Role of the Editor

'One who prepares the work of others for publication; one who conducts or manages a newspaper.'
(Concise English Dictionary)

There is no doubt that an editor is a key player in any newspaper operation and these days they can become minor celebrities (e.g. Piers Morgan of *The Mirror* and *The Sunday Mirror*; Rebekah Wade of the *News of the World*) who are consulted for their opinion by other media.

A fundamental responsibility for the editor is to act as a 'gatekeeper', filtering and restricting what news actually appears within each publication. Their role can, therefore, be considered within our study of news values and news selection since they very clearly determine the news agenda of their publication. Indeed their decisions on what is selected for publication is often the basis for news stories in themselves.

One person who illustrates this extremely well is Rebekah Wade, the editor of the *News of the World*. Wade is Fleet Street's youngest editor, working in a male-dominated environment; however she has not shied away from controversy since joining the tabloid (from *The Sun*, where she was Deputy Editor). In the summer of 2000 she published the names and photographs of 50 convicted sex offenders at a time when the media (and therefore the nation) were focusing on the problem of reintegrating known paedophiles back into the community. Wade also gave the green light for the publication of the 'Sophiegate' tape transcripts, the recorded interviews with Sophie of Wessex, in April 2001 - a decision she took knowing the embarrassment that this would cause the Royal family, as the interviews included personal comments about some members of the family, her marriage to Prince Edward and the Prime Minister, Tony Blair. Both of these decisions became news stories in their own right, resulting in the newspaper itself, as well as the stories, becoming headline news.

According to Tunstall (1996), editors are 'activist entrepreneurs' who are involved with the following tasks:

• Hiring and firing personnel.

• The formation of opinion through developing the newspaper's formal policy as well as via selecting (or rejecting) articles, letters and cartoons to be published within their publication.

• They manage the editorial budget.

• They are involved on the gathering of news and features and they chair the meetings where decisions are made regarding publication.

• They are involved in the processing of the news and features.

• They contribute towards the decisions made over the newspaper presentation and design.

• They manage systems.

• They write certain sections of the newspaper.

• They are involved with the newspaper's promotion and marketing strategy.

All of these elements are particularly true in tabloids since in broadsheet newspapers (e.g. *The Times*) there is often a team of editors – an Executive Editor who oversees the whole operation, a Deputy Editor, a Managing Editor and two or three Assistant Editors.

An editor is not only the purveyor of the in-house style – and thereby operating a form of self-censorship – but she or he is responsible for speaking on behalf of their readers – the consensual 'we'. This is especially true of their editorials which claim to speak to, and for, their readers and often proclaim forth on issues such as patriotism, moral fortitude and industry. They allow the newspaper to comment about everyday events and are overtly opinionated (e.g. *Daily Mirror* Comment; *The Daily Star* Says). The editor addresses the audience directly in a style that assumes that they share those opinions and values (i.e. there is an 'implied reader').

As the key decision-maker for the newspaper, the editor can be held responsible for any effect that an article may have as a result of it being published; ultimately they are entirely culpable and can be imprisoned if it is deemed a severe enough case (e.g. as early as January 1808, the editor of *The Examiner*, Leigh Hunt, was imprisoned for publishing criticism of the Prince Regent). This is particularly true when it relates to a court case. In the early 1950s, the then editor of *The Daily Mirror*, Sylvester Bolam, was imprisoned for three months in Brixton prison for its pre-trial coverage of the trial of murderer John Haigh. Haigh had killed a number of old ladies by strangulation and then disposed of their bodies in an acid bath. He had attempted to plea insanity as he believed that he had Transylvanian ancestors. Bolam was the last editor to be sent to prison - and unfortunately he died aged 47, shortly after serving his sentence. (Ironically it was about this time that the first Royal Commission on the Press was established, which set out a proposal for the Press Council which was to come into being in the late 1950s.)

These days any editor who is believed to have over-stepped the mark is 'encouraged' to resign over the matter as it is considered unreasonable for them to reside over editorial decisions any longer. A recent example of this is the *Sunday Mirror's* editor Colin Myler, who paid the price for publishing an article in April 2001 which led to the collapse of a high profile, multi-million pound court case which focused on Lee Bowyer and Jonathan Woodgate, a couple of Leeds United football players who had been accused of assaulting an Asian student; he departed within days of his 'serious error of judgment'. This is also a good example of when tabloids not only report the news but also make it themselves.

Gatekeeping:

This is an extremely important term to explore when considering the tabloid press as it is inextricably bound up with the notion that the content of a newspaper (and a television broadcast) is manipulated in some way; the content, and the order of that content, is predetermined for the audience resulting in their opinions being skewed in favour of what they are led to believe.

The term 'gatekeeper' was coined by D. M. White and implies that the person who determines the content and the order of a mass medium form of communication 'opens the gate' to certain news items, channels of communication and pieces of information and 'closes the gate' to the rest. This fundamental consequence of this action is that what we see or read is a highly selective view of reality (and is therefore arguably a distorted, somewhat skewed view).

In the newspaper industry the gatekeepers are the editors and the sub-editors, and their role as gatekeeper is inextricably bound up with the news production process: the news flows from the original event to the newspaper office via the journalist or the public and the information is edited and made to fit the format of the newspaper. There is another layer of gatekeeping which occurs when the newspaper's readers receive the news; they do not necessarily read every news item and only remember certain aspects of each item as again a layer of selection and editing has occurred.

Dennis MacShane (1979) saw this news production process as being divided into three distinct stages:
1. gathering
2. selecting
3. treating.

MacShane believed that the gatekeeping role was particularly pertinent at the third stage of this process and that a fundamental flaw was that at each stage of gatekeeping people earlier on in the chain were unaware of those changes being made.

Agenda setting:

The editor of any publication actively determines which items of news and therefore which issues are of the most important to their readers by virtue of the fact that they select them for their newspaper. A consequence of this decision-making process (i.e. limiting or constraining what the readers have access to/knowledge of) is that these news items, when consumed by the readers, become their news agenda for that day; these are the topics that the readers discuss with relatives, friends and work colleagues. The content of tabloids has an emphasis on domestic news stories so this sets the news agenda within the confines of the reader's own country (other countries are covered when, for example, they are having an election which may effect the UK, if they are suffering from a large-scale disaster, if there is a key sporting event which involves a British team or a Royal family member is visiting there).

To a certain extent newspapers can be said to reflect the ideas, beliefs and values of the majority, particularly as they are a mass media product. However, their knowledge of the consensus is limited and so the reality is that they decide what we are supposed to sign up to since they determine what we receive and how we receive it.

The Sub-editor

It is important to distinguish the sub-editor from the editor as both have areas of responsibility that are fundamental to a newspaper. The sub-editor's key tasks can be defined as follows:

- Involved in decisions about the news values/'taste' of news items.

- Decide on what stories go on which page.

- Do a spelling and grammar check.

- Write the headlines.*

- Edit stories to fit the page.

- Ensure that the type is the same size.

- Ensure that stories have an attention-grabbing intro.**

- Ensure that each page keeps to its deadline (to the minute).

Sub-editors have to work with the news pieces that have been passed onto them. For these pieces they must find an angle which they think their readers will be interested

*The golden rule of headlines is that they have to be in the present tense and not include 'is', 'an' or 'a'.

**Journalists work on the assumption that the average person spends 30 minutes reading their newspaper, so the convention is to include the '5W's' in the first paragraph of each story – Who? What? Where? When? Why? - to guarantee that the reader gets the facts immediately in the hope that they will want to read on.

in and ensure that it conforms to the in-house style. It must be presented in a way that will be the most effective and attention grabbing. Clearly the issue of gatekeeping is valid here as the way in which a sub-editor adapts the content and layout of the piece will largely depend on their own opinions and individual taste.

Newspaper Proprietors

Alongside the employees of a newspaper it is important to consider the role of the person(s) who actually owns the publication (or group of publications). Clearly, within a free press ownership is a significant factor. The proprietor of the newspaper is the legal owner and therefore is ultimately accountable for the newspaper. The extent to which their individual political persuasion is brought to bare upon the content and in-house style is an interesting point to consider; as the owner of the newspaper their political stance will inevitably be a primary influence.

One thing that is certain is that newspaper proprietors are often male entrepreneurs who have their fingers in a lot of media pies and the number of actual newspaper owners is becoming increasingly small with a number of different titles (broadsheet and tabloid) owned by a small number of competing newspaper groups.

Case study: Rupert Murdoch (a.k.a. 'the Napoleon of modern media' *The Guardian)*

'He breaks the rules sometimes of gentlemanly conduct, and he's made a career out of doing that.'
Thomas Kiernan, *biographer*
(from the video *Who's Afraid of Rupert Murdoch?*)

* Keith Rupert Murdoch
* Born 11 March 1931, Melbourne, Australia
* Married to second wife, Wendy Deng
* Lives in Soho, Manhattan, USA

Newspaper publisher and media entrepreneur; founder and head of the global holding company The News Corporation Ltd (which governed News Ltd, Australia; News International, UK; News America Holdings Inc., USA). Today, News Corp. (of which Murdoch is the Chair and CEO) has total assets of $4.3 billion and it includes the lion's share of newspapers in Australia, approximately one third of British newspapers and BSkyB and businesses in most media industries across three continents.

Murdoch's corporate interests mean that he has ventured into newspaper, magazine, book and electronic publishing, television broadcasting, film and video production mainly in the USA, the UK and his native Australia.

The son of Sir Keith Murdoch, a famous Australian war correspondent and publisher, Murdoch studied at Worcester College, Oxford and briefly worked as the editor of Lord Beaverbrook's London *Daily Express* where he gained an excellent grounding in sensationalist journalism, believing that newspapers were meant to entertain, not educate. He returned to Australia in 1952 when his father died to assume control of his inheritance – *The Adelaide News* and *Sunday Mail* – changing their style to reflect the 'sex and scandal' style that he had learnt during his time at the helm of the *Express*. As a result of this change in content the sales figures soared and he proceeded to do the same to newspapers he went on to take over in Sydney, Perth, Melbourne and Brisbane.

At this time – 1969 - he also acquired his first British newspaper, the *News of the World*, which at the time was Britain's biggest-selling newspaper. The Carr family had run the paper since 1891 and Murdoch beat off the competition in the form of Robert Maxwell for the paper (despite Maxwell offering a larger bid). Murdoch promised that he wouldn't seek majority ownership but after acquiring the paper he reneged on this and sought majority control. Murdoch soon set about applying his proven winning formula, namely an emphasis on crime, sex, scandal and human interest stories, bold headlines, prolific sports reporting and outspoken conservative (and Conservative) editorialising; the paper gained the nickname the 'News of the Screws'. Murdoch acquired *The Sun* in 1970 and adapted it to fit the same pattern as the *News of the World*, adding a new touch, the 'Sun Lovely', a topless model on Page 3. Interestingly, their right-wing political formula continued until the general election of 1997 when the two newspapers changed their allegiance to support the newly elected Labour Party.

Some of the major Murdoch ventures through the decades are as follows:

Title	Decade in which he took over/introduced
Adelaide News	1950s
The Mirror, Sydney, *The News of the World* and *The Sun*, London *The Australian*	1960s
San Antonio News (renamed *Express News*) *The New York Post*	1970s
Herald American (renamed *Boston Herald*), *Chicago Sun-Times* *TV Guide, The Times, The Sunday Times*, London 20th Century Fox, USA, Fox TV, USA	1980s
Star TV, Asia	1990s

According to Andrew Neil (former editor of *The Sunday Times*), Murdoch's acquisition of *The Times* should have been referred to the Monopolies Commission (since he also owned *The Sun* and the *News of the World*) but this was avoided as Murdoch had the right political connections. Nevertheless, the Parliament's Articles of Association do assert that Murdoch is not allowed to be involved with any editorial direction that *The Times* takes.

Murdoch became an American citizen in 1985 and in the late 1980s and 90s diversified and amassed major holdings in other communication ventures. In 1985 he acquired 20th Century Fox Film Corp. and bought several independent American television stations from Metromedia Inc., consolidating both of these ventures into Fox Inc. He bought the Australian news groups *The Herald* and *Weekly News* Ltd in 1987 and then bought into several book-publishing companies such as Harper and Row Publishers in 1987, Zondervan (a religious book publisher) in 1988, Scott, Foresman and Co. (a textbook and trade publisher) in 1989 and in the UK William Collins Ltd in 1989. These publishing acquisitions were merged, together with some operations in Australia and New Zealand, to become HarperCollins publishers in 1990.

A similar merger occurred when Murdoch's Sky Television, a four-channel satellite service which he had established in 1989, merged with its rival British Satellite Broadcasting in 1990 to become BSkyB. (The debt incurred from this heavy expansion exercise was offset by his selling off *New York*, *Seventeen* and *Daily Racing Form*, together with several American magazines.) In 1993 he acquired Star-TV (a pan-Asian television service in Hong Kong) in an attempt to build his global television network presence and in 1995 he merged News Corporation with MCI Communications Corp., a long-distance telecommunications service provider in the USA. Murdoch also owns the Los Angeles Dodgers baseball team (he bought them for a cool $350 million in May 1997), the National Rugby League; Fox Interactive and his own LineOne Service.

RUPERT MURDOCH

'Can we change the world? No, but hell we can all try.'
Rupert Murdoch
(Askmen.com)

As if to illustrate the ambivalence in which he is held, the following two extracts, by the same author, show how Murdoch's business activities can be interpreted differently:

'It is a truth universally acknowledged that Rupert Murdoch is scum. The media tycoon has built his empire on shlock and sleaze, used heavy handed tactics and legal chicanery to evade laws and taxes, toppled British and Australian governments to expand his domain, all but bribed Newt Gingrich and Margaret Thatcher with sweetheart book deals, made mockery of the grand traditions of Australian/British/American journalism. He is perhaps the world's most sinister businessman, the Ernst Blofeld of the Information Age. Even his company's name, News Corp., has an ominous Big Brother ring to it.'
(David Plotz, MSN Web site home page, posted 24 May 1997)

'He has done more to help the great mass of media consumers than anyone ... Murdoch is the global capitalist par excellence, the very model of free enterprise and entrepreneurship. Almost single-handedly, Murdoch has modernized the world's media, forcing competition on stagnant businesses, cracking open monopolies and oligopolies, vanquishing 'traditions' that were often an excuse for laziness, unleashing the creative destruction of capitalism on an industry that thought itself exempt ... everywhere Murdoch has gone, competition, efficiency, and consumer choice (and profit) have followed.'
(David Plotz, MSN Web site home page, posted 24 May 1997)

Freedom of the Press

The issue of immunity from government control of any form of censorship is a fundamental one when considering the work of the journalist and the role of the press within a democratic society. Clearly the media is a powerful, autonomous institution that acts as a key communicator and has the power to support or criticise the government. However, we must also be aware that this independence can lead to abuse of power with newspapers frequently overstepping the mark, undermining people and invading their privacy.

The press in Britain has enjoyed relative freedom from government intervention since the eighteenth century. In the twenty-first century control over the press is achieved almost entirely through self-regulation with the majority of newspapers adhering to a Code of Practice which was established by the Press Complaints Commision (PCC) and a group of editors in 1991 as a system for adjudication for complaints. This system relies on the co-operation of the newspapers and has no coercive powers.

Concern about the press abusing their power, particularly when it comes to invasion of the personal lives of key societal people such as politicians and the Monarchy, led to the establishment of the Calcutt Committee. The Committee reported in January 1993 that the notion of self-regulation had failed and that a new system should be devised which would replace the existing one. The singular most important recommendation of the Committee was that the press should adhere to a statutory Complaints Tribunal that would be chaired by a judge or a senior lawyer. The tribunal would wield a number of key powers including the power to order an apology,

An interesting case study to consider is the trial of those accused of the murder, of black teenager Stephen Lawrence. The case was the subject of much media attention as the media implied that the murder was racially motivated. This was exacerbated by the Daily Mail's decision to publish the names of the five men accused, but later acquitted, of Stephen's murder and challenging the men to sue the newspaper if they were innocent.

The Lawrence family welcomed the tabloid's decision but others criticised the move as a 'trial by media': by publishing the names of the young white men and issuing them a challenge the newspaper was implying that they were guilty and therefore encouraging their readers to think likewise, despite the court's judgment. Nigel Pascoe, QC, chair of the Bar Council's Public Affairs Committee, said at the time, 'It is not for the press to act as judge and jury'. **(The Times, 15 February 1997).**

compensation or fines. The Committee also recommended the establishment of criminal and civil offences regarding the method by which journalists acquired their information (e.g. unlawful entry to private property). The Committee also urged the government to create a privacy tort.

Control of the press in other countries

Countries with a written constitution often contain special dispensation for press freedom. In the USA, the First Amendment confers constitutional status to press freedom that means that the journalists, writers and publishers are able to criticise the government and are free from censorship. Similarly, in Canada the Charter of Rights and Freedoms gives constitutional protection to the press. The USA, Canada, Australia and New Zealand also have specific legislation protecting freedom of information. This facilitates an openness in reporting key issues and events.

A useful way of comparing the different constitutional systems of protection is to look at the law of defamation. The English legal system is much more likely to issue an injunction to prevent publication of an alleged libel. In the USA the Supreme Court asserts that under the First Amendment (which protects freedom of the press) liability is restricted to cases where a libel has been made maliciously whereas in England libel is a tort of strict liability.

Article 10 of the European Convention on Human Rights protects the freedom to receive and impart information and ideas without interference by public authority. The UK adheres to this and is therefore influenced by constitutional protections for press freedom.

Free speech versus privacy

The line between the right to free speech (or what news-papers would call 'in the public interest') and the right to privacy is at the best of times a thin one, particularly for journalists whose fundamental motivation is to write a story which 'sells' (in other words boosts circulation figures). Newspapers (and arguably tabloids more than most) have a reductionist interpretation of what is in the public's interest in their pursuit of a commercial impera-tive. The issue of privacy has become a hot topic recently following the first legal case in Britain to appeal to the right to privacy enshrined in the European convention. Ironically the case was brought to court by a couple who are rarely out of the limelight – Catherine Zeta-Jones and Michael Douglas – who had signed a deal with *OK!* magazine granting them the exclusive rights to photo-graph their wedding. However, *Hello!* magazine (*OK!'s* arch rival) published some photos taken by a concealed camera at the wedding, three days before *OK!* hit the news stands. Zeta-Jones and Douglas sued for breach of privacy and the court of appeal upheld their action.

What should journalists cover? What should we, the public, be made aware of? What do we have a right to know? Where does the responsibility for this decision-making-cum-censorship rest? Clearly the boundaries of acceptability are a subjective topic and are according to the British constitution subject to the parameters of the law.

A number of useful case studies follow which demon-strate the precarious and, ironically, headline grabbing nature of the thin line that exists between the right to free speech and the right to privacy.

Case study 1: Television actress Amanda Holden vs *The Star* – June 2001

No stranger to the attention of the tabloid press, Holden was somewhat irked when *The Star* published a double-page spread of some long-lens photographs of her sunbathing topless, with her hair in rollers, while holidaying with her husband in Tuscany, accompanied by the headline 'It's Miss Titley in the Garden of Eden' (a reference to a character she plays in the ITV sitcom *The Grimleys*). The newspaper accompanied the photos with a piece which retold the story of Holden's extra-marital affair and promised to print more photos the following day but was prevented from doing so as Holden won an ex-parte injunction (i.e. it was granted in the absence of *The Star*, with the judge hearing one side of the story only) against the newspaper, accusing them of acting in breach of Clause 3 of the PCC's Code of Practice which outlaws long-lens pictures taken on private property, unless it is in the public interest.

In seeking a fast resolution, Holden had not gone down the conventional path of contacting the PCC but had gone straight to the courts via her solicitor, Peter Crawford of Stitt and Co., claiming damages from the paper for the photos which had been taken by an agency and were not sanctioned by her. Holden's claim against the newspaper was reinforced by the incorporation of the Human Rights Act into English law and her claim was made all the more speedy by side-stepping the PCC, who could not have acted so quickly.

The Star's response was to apologise for the lack of a second instalment of the promised photos and replace it with pictures of Page 3 stalwart Jordan. The apology read:

'Miss Titley's boobs: unfortunately, due to a bit of legal wrangling, we are unable to bring you more of Amanda Holden's finest assets today, but the case continues. Enjoy Jordan's instead!'

Holden took the temporary injunction further, however, and together with her husband, Les Dennis, served a forty page writ on *The Star* demanding a promise not to publish the pictures again and sought damages from the newspaper.

The interesting point here is that the PCC was side-stepped, but their Code of Practice was cited in the claim made against the newspaper. At the time of writing the case is awaiting trial.

Case study 2: Stephen Gately in harmony with *The Sun* – June 1999

In a somewhat crass bid to win new readers in January 1999, *The Sun* boasted that it was 'The Paper That Loves Poofs' (a charming sales booster). So it was no real surprise that in June 1999 the editor, David Yelland, decided to carry the world exclusive that teen heart-throb and boy band superstar, Stephen Gately (singer with the mega-successful Boyzone) was gay. However, contrary to what one might expect of a tabloid this was not the usual 'outing' of a high profile celeb (like that of former well-loved, now disgraced television personality Michael Barrymore). The story had the full consent and approval of the man in question, though the motivation behind the 'outing' was the same - sales.

Boyzone's publicists, Outside Organisation, had heard that a former roadie with the band was about to leak the story to the press and amidst fear about how the devoted teen fans might handle the revelation about their teen idol, they decided to work with *The Sun* (who had been enormously supportive of the band up to now) to publish the story. The band wanted the story to be handled with sensitivity and so they worked closely with Yelland to get it right, with Yately having a total say on what was written (he even gave them a photograph of his partner, Eloy de Jong, to publish).

Yelland's carefulness about printing the story was also connected to his recent caution from the PCC over his decision in May 1999 to publish topless photos of Sophie Rhys-Jones (then girlfriend, now wife of Prince Edward): Yelland's need to be accurate was never more so. However, Yately approved the final copy and the story was published under the headline, 'Boyzone Stephen: I'm gay and in love' with the details of the band's Web site chat room published for distressed fans to log on to.

Interestingly, and ironically, *The Mirror* published a story the next day in response to this exclusive which gave an interview with Stephen's mother, Margaret, who, according to *The Mirror* felt that Stephen had been black-mailed into telling his story.

Case study 3: The news coverage concerning the child killers of James Bulger

When the horrific details of toddler James Bulger's death (battered to death on a railway line in Liverpool) were reported in the media in February 1992, the two ten-year-old boys responsible, Jon Venables and Robert Thompson, incurred the collective wrath of the general public who were mortified that such young boys could be capable of such an act. The lengths that some newspapers went to in order to print CCTV images of James's last movements and describe his last hours at the hands of the two boys, guaranteed that the story would survive in the public memory for quite some time. Indeed, when it was announced, following a decision by Chief Justice Lord Woolf, that Venables and Thompson, would be released in June 2001 having served eight years and four months on secure units, the press spent some time speculating on what they would look like now and where they would live, ensuring that once again the public were reminded of their crime and endangering the lives of the two young men and their families. Headlines such as 'Crazy' (*The Sun*) and 'This Disgusts Me' (*The Mirror*) guaranteed it remained high on the tabloid agenda. Such was the court's concern over potential revenge attacks (the boys had already received numerous death threats), that Venables and Thompson were granted new names and their identities were only known to a very small number of officials.

To try to ensure that this remained the case and the two young men were protected, a court order – the first lifetime media injunction made against the English and Welsh media –was granted by Dame Elizabeth Butler-Sloss, a senior high court judge, in January 2001 to protect the young men's identities and their whereabouts. Similarly, the Home Secretary, David Blunkett, wrote to a number of publications on the Continent, in an attempt to persuade them to desist from publishing any recent photos.

Three newspaper groups – the owners of *The Mirror*, the *Daily Mail*, *The Sun* and the *News of the World* - all went to court to try and oppose the imposition as they felt it inhibited press freedom, but the decision to impose a 'gag' remained intact. Despite the court's measures, *The Manchester Evening News* allegedly failed to adhere to the injunction and published the whereabouts of Venables and Thompson (at the time of going to press the court is yet to make a decision on the case). Nevertheless, with tabloid headlines such as 'Bulger Killers Better Off Dead' (*Daily Star*); 'Bulger Killer Dead in Four Weeks' (*News of the World*) and former Tory MP David Mellor chipping in with 'Kill a kid and get a house' in *The People*, it's a safe bet that this story will continue to dominate the British press: while the public's appetite for the story is still keen, the press will continue to write what sells.

The furore surrounding their release is reminiscent of the case of Mary Bell, who killed two babies when she was eleven. Upon release, at the age of twenty-three, she was eligible for protection from the British press because she had a daughter. Nevertheless, the tabloids broke the injunction unceremoniously in 1998 when they printed photographs of the daughter who was by then fourteen-years-old.

In the case of children who have been found guilty of murder there are three key reasons for banning reporting on them:
1. protecting the offenders to ensure that some people do not take the law into their own hands (some might argue that press coverage actually incites this);

2. the offenders' right to privacy as laid down in the new Human Rights Act;

3. protecting the public to ensure that the offenders are adequately rehabilitated.

'Bring Me 150 Babies!'
Case study: the air-lifted Vietnamese orphans and the publicity–hungry tabloid editor

In April 1975, the *Daily Mail* was run by an extremely proactive editor – David English - whose ethos was not simply to report news but to make it; he saw publicity stunts as a way of 'forging closer links with current readers and attracting new ones' (*The Guardian*, 6 August 2001). At this time a terrible war was being waged in the Vietcong and there was a fear that once the US withdrew their troops, the communists would set about destroying the enormous number of Vietnamese refugees. (This theory had certainly been perpetuated by the American press.) In a propagandist bid to help alleviate the situation (and in the face of defeat) US President Ford pledged that he would rescue 2,000 children by air. The *Daily Mail's* foreign editor, Brian Freemantle, suggested to David English that he did the same. English thought that this was an excellent idea and announced his intention to the nation the best way that he knew how – on the front page. In his editorial he spoke of offering these Vietnamese children 'a raft of hope ... in the seas of despair'.

Not only was this a brilliant coup for the newspaper but English himself was doing what the British government wasn't – he was taking action against the communists and was placing himself on a level with President Ford. The tabloid's readers were so inspired by the paper's intention that donations started to flood in; over £50,000 was donated. It seemed that the tabloid had successfully appealed to the white middle-class values of its core readership.

Once in Vietnam the journalists hit on a problem – they couldn't gather enough babies to fulfil their promise of 150 baby orphans and they hadn't considered the fact that it usually took two years to get children out of Vietnam. In an attempt to get 150 children, the journalists sent the word around to a number of adoption agencies and charities and by the time the *Mail*'s plane arrived there were 99 children, 22 of whom were not babies as had been the initial pledge, but were aged between 5 and 14, and some of whom were not actually orphans, but whose parents had handed them over on what they had believed was a temporary basis, to people who they thought could offer better treatment than they could during the crisis. During the airlift many of the younger babies whose identity was unknown had a number crayoned on their back, but in the sweltering heat this was rubbed off and so they remained unidentified upon arrival.

Naturally, the *Mail* dedicated 6 pages to the airlift, indeed the journalists telephoned in their copy to central office whilst the plane re-fuelled in Dubai, to ensure that it made the front page on 6 April. In the words of Freemantle, '… to use a journalistic cliché, it wrote itself'. The newspaper justified the shortfall in numbers by the necessity to act quickly due to the ill health of many of the 'orphans' – 'in Britain, all these 100 [it was actually 99] orphans will be given a chance to live and a chance to be loved.' English chose to have a picture of himself carrying one of the children alongside a story which focused on how he had overcome problems with airport officials who had, at first refused the plane permission to leave. Another report carried the headline, 'Why didn't the cabinet act?' – the paper's political intentions were explicit. While the photo of English with a child in his arms appeared on page 3 of the newspaper; a similar photo of President Ford with a child in his arms was left 'til page 4. The next day the newspaper reported that 6 children had already been adopted, 34 remained in hospital, and the remaining 54 were sent to reception homes.

The newsworthiness of the story was bled dry by the tabloid with the story being covered for days and days; the paper fully intended to get their money's worth from their actions and in response to questions about his motives English denied that it had all been a publicity-seeking adventure, claiming that it had been a 'great newspaper enterprise … if it was publicity that saved those children's lives, then I am proud to think we engendered that publicity.' (*The Guardian*, 6 August 2001).

Twenty-one years later in 1996 the story was still considered newsworthy and the tabloid, predictably, focused on the success of its actions, extolling the virtues of their mission, reporting that many of the children had gone on to university and good jobs; indeed 17 of the original orphans were sent back to Saigon, at the tabloid's expense, for the very first time. What the paper didn't tell its readers was that only 51 of the 99 children had gone on to be adopted, the rest had either gone to special homes or had never left the home to which they had originally been sent. Nor did they report on how, for many of the children, particularly those who had not been babies and therefore had some memory of living in Vietnam and their families, the decision to remove them, permanently, had had life long consequences. The reality is that only two have ever made contact with their families.

*More information on this story can be found at **www.channel4.com/plus** in a section that focuses on a documentary Children of the Airlift which Channel 4 screened on 9 August 2001. The story is also featured in Roy Greenslade's forthcoming book 'Profits From Propaganda' which will be published by MacMillan in 2002.*

'Bin the Whingers'

The Mirror published a list of rules under the headline 'Bin the Whingers' (1 August 2001) as a result of their annoyance at celebrities' complaints about their privacy being invaded by the press on the one hand, and yet selling their story when it suited them, on the other. This alleged hypocrisy led the tabloid to devise their own set of rules which were akin to the fouling system used in football and would be used to place celebrities in the newspaper's 'Celebrity Sin Bin': 'we'll bin them and ban them … cutting off their oxygen of publicity'.

The following is an extract from the article:

Rules:
Celebrities who incur our yellow card will be banned from *The Mirror* for a week.

Some ways to get a yellow card:
- Moaning about being bothered by fans when out in public.
- Complaining about being photographed in the street, on a beach or on the high seas.
- Inviting a glossy mag into your home to discuss your personal life and then whingeing about press intrusion when the bad times hit.

Celebrities who incur our red card will be banned from *The Mirror* for a month.

Some ways to get a red card:
- For exploiting a personal occasion, i.e. a marriage, to promote a new product – i.e. a chocolate bar
- For assaulting a member of the media in a public place without provocation.
- For going to the European Court of Human Rights when you've been caught bang to rights.

Institutions

The following organisations represent key media institutions that are connected to the press in some way, be it in a regulatory capacity or an audience-monitoring role. Newspapers, by comparison to other media, are reasonably unrestricted insofar as anyone can own one so long as they print the publisher's name on each issue and they cannot contravene certain laws (defamation, official secrecy, contempt of court, race relations, etc.). Similarly, if their circulation exceeds 500,000 they must seek Department of Trade approval; it is rarely withheld. Nevertheless, newspapers are costly (£10 million according to the 1991 Sadler Enquiry) and it is this fact which virtually guarantees a monopoly by a few.

Key Media Institutions

Press Complaints Commission (PCC)

Established in 1991 and funded entirely by the newspaper industry, this is an independent regulatory body which works within the realms of journalism to handle the issue of standards. The PCC's President is Lord Wakeham (since 1995) and 16 members assist him: a Chair, public members (who are not able to have any connection with press business) and press members (who must be experienced at senior editorial level).

Many laws govern the content of newspapers but not the behaviour or methods by which stories are achieved by journalists. There is no statutory regulation of the press but there is a voluntary system, a Code of Practice, which does not have the force of the law but has been drawn up by the industry which funds the PCC to resolve or adjudicate any complaints received on issues such as inaccuracy, privacy, misrepresentation and harassment; they do not tackle the broader issues of press freedom. The PCC does, however, give general guidance to editors on related ethical issues.

As a rule, editors agree to publish the PCC's criticisms but damages cannot be awarded when fault is found. (You can register comments about the industry's Code of Practice with the Code of Practice Committee.) The PCC receives several thousand complaints a year with the majority citing unfairness or inaccuracy as their grievance. Prior to the formation of the PCC, there was a voluntary Press Council that existed for some 40 years and was generally considered a toothless watchdog. The PCC was established after concern about press standards, particularly within the 'gutter press' (i.e. the tabloids). Concern over invasion of privacy was particularly levelled at the tabloids over their rather unscrupulous coverage of the Royal family and certain politicians; what they considered to be in the public interest was not a universally held belief. After some pressure, the then Tory Government appointed Sir David Calcutt to undertake a Departmental Committee of Enquiry who reported back in 1990, recommending the establishment of a non-statutory Press Complaints Commission, which would function for an initial trial period of 18 months to see if it would work. If it failed then the government would be coerced into passing legislation. The PCC was hurriedly assembled to avoid any unwanted legislative controls.

In the past the PCC has come under fire from Parliament who deemed that it was draconian in its judgments and ineffective as a regulator (this was especially true of another report undertaken by Calcutt in 1993). In recent years the work of the PCC has come under scrutiny, especially over the coverage of the Royal family (most notably the death of Diana, Princess of Wales, when the paparazzi were widely believed to have been responsible for causing the fatal car crash; indeed her brother, Lord

Spencer, publicly accused every editor who had ever paid for sensational photos of Diana of having 'blood on their hands'). Some people raised the question of whether the code was a sufficiently strong mechanism to control the press. However, a consequence of the circumstances surrounding the death of Diana has led to the Code being revised and, under the guidance of Lord Wakeham, the PCC has enjoyed renewed faith in its abilities, particularly over the treatment and media coverage of the Royal family and celebrities; indeed Prince William was guest of honour at the PCC's tenth anniversary celebrations. (How's that for an ironic photo opportunity?)

Nevertheless, the fact still remains that the PCC acts as a conciliator rather than a judge and that the newspapers' obligation to publish a correction or an apology is a small price to pay compared to those who may have genuinely suffered as a consequence of material published within newspapers.

National Readership Survey (NRS)

The National Readership Survey is a non-profit making commercial organisation which is the largest provider of an estimate of the number and nature (i.e. the size and quality) of the people who read UK newspapers (and consumer magazines). Conducted by Research Services Ltd, the NRS provides the following people with information:

- editors with an up-to-date description of the readers reached by their publication;
- publishers of newspapers and magazines with the data they need to sell advertising space;
- advertisers/advertising agencies with the information necessary for them to plan/buy advertising space.

This information is acquired via an annual subscription by the newspaper, magazine or advertiser to their relevant industry association.

Approximately 250 publications use this readership data to look at readership totals as well as a detailed profile of their readers in terms of their sex, age, income, employment and where they live. The NRS can also (to a limited extent) provide information on what car or credit card the readers own, and who supplies their electricity and gas. The information is achieved via the surveys of 35,000 people in a face-to-face interview and is updated on a monthly basis in an attempt to gain an accurate reflection. Most publishers, however, use the information on a quarterly basis to illustrate six-monthly or annual figures.

Target Group Index (TGI)

This is research, conducted by the British Market Research Bureau (BMRB), that provides a much more detailed market analysis than the NRS for a smaller number of publications (approximately 180). The research covers socio-demographic information as well as areas such as fast-moving consumer goods, banking, cars, airlines and holidays (4,000+ brands in over 500 fields are covered). Statistics are determined via questionnaires that are distributed to over 25,000 people. The results are published annually with a six-monthly update available.

The Premier TGI is the up-market version of this research. Conducted by the BMRB the research focuses closely on people who come within the AB social classes. The research is published annually and based in the responses of 5,700 people.

Campaign for Press and Broadcasting Freedom (CPBF)

'Campaigning for a diverse, democratic and accountable media.'
(CPBF publicity leaflet)

Established in 1979, this is an independent group that seeks to promote policies for a democratically accountable media. Work that they do includes: initiating debate and lobbying MP's on issues such as the right to reply and the future of the local press; producing a bi-monthly magazine for its members; conducting and supporting research which explores media issues; publishing books, pamphlets and guides to assist people who wish to express an opinion in the media; engaging speakers for political events, trade unions, schools etc.; and organising an annual conference which focuses on a topical media issue.

Some of the key issues which the CPBF actively campaign for in relation to the press are the following:

- The establishment of a statutory 'right of reply' to factual inaccuracies. A body which would be established to promote the interests of readers, viewers and listeners and would administer the right of reply and represent their interests as media consumers.

- The repeal of certain legislation (1981 Contempt of Court Act; 1986 Police and Criminal Evidence Act; 1994 Criminal Justice Act) which restricts the rights of the journalist to report.

- Proposals for a review of the libel laws which encourage the implementation of a fast-track service which would be free for ordinary people to gain redress.

- The incorporation of the European Convention on Human Rights into UK law which would allow for the right of privacy and to freedom of expression.

- Contractual protection against interference with their professional standards by proprietors or editors; they should be free to refuse to handle copy which breaches the NUJ Code of Conduct or the Industry Code of Practice.

- The imposition of effective controls to limit the spread of cross-media ownership and to ensure pluralism of ownership.

- The passing of a Freedom of Information Act which opens up government papers to journalistic and public scrutiny.

- A reform of the 1989 Official Secrets Act to alter the prohibitions on what can be reported and to strengthen the public interest defence. In addition, abolition of the 'D' notice system.

National Union of Journalists (NUJ)

The NUJ is the world's largest trade union for journalists, with over 25,000 members across the United Kingdom. In the UK it is affiliated to the TUC and the GFTU, it is also affiliated to the International Federation of Journalists. The union has an Ethics Council that investigates whether its members have breached its Code and has had a Code of Conduct for its members since 1936. In the UK it was a founder member of the Creators' Copyright Coalition, a forum that advocates the co-operation of all creators' organisations. The union offers advice and support for its members, publishes a newsletter, consults on policy and planning, and organises regular branch and national meetings/conferences.

PressWise

A non-profit making limited liability company, which was established in 1993 by 'victims of press abuse' and is backed by sympathetic journalists and media lawyers concerned with media ethics. It seeks to improve journalistic practice and public understanding of mass media by offering advice, information and training courses, particularly for those who have been on the receiving end of inaccurate, intrusive or sensational press coverage. In their pamphlet it states:

'we provide advice to those affected by unfair or inaccurate media coverage [and] ... assert the public's right to receive accurate information. We regard press freedom as a responsibility exercised by journalists on behalf of the public, not a licence to make money.'

Audit Bureau of Circulation (ABC)

Established in 1931 to provide advertisers with circulation figures. The Bureau is comprised of advertisers, advertising agencies and publishers and is a non-profit making organisation. Circulation figures are published once a month alongside a six-monthly rolling average.

Media Guardian Top 100

On 16 July 2001, the media supplement in *The Guardian* newspaper published a list of the top 100 people who 'decide what you watch, read, hear or download'. The list was based on information available within the public domain so if figures weren't known (e.g. someone's salary) then they were omitted and not approximated.

The criteria for selection were as follows:

• Cultural influence;

• Economic power;

• Political power.

Several individuals who play an integral role within the tabloid press featured in the list. A total of 15 such people – proprietors, editors and those who work for businesses who have a direct relationship with the press (e.g. PCC, Reuters, Labour Party) – were represented. Below is a summary of *The Guardian's* findings:

Name/rank in list	Job turnover	Company value/Circ.	Staff	Age/ annual salary
Rupert Murdoch/1	Chairman, News Corporation	£16.5bn	34,000	70/£2.3m
Paul Dacre/8	Group editor of Associated Newspapers and Editor of the *Daily Mail*	Daily Mail & General Trust £959.5m	Associated Newspapers 2,500; Daily Mail & General Trust 18,675	52/£727,000
David Yelland/14	Editor, *The Sun*	Circulation 3.5m	?	38/£?
Piers Morgan/19	Editor in chief, *Daily Mirror* & *Sunday Mirror*	£1bn	14,000	36/£300,000
Philip Graf/20	Chief Executive, Trinity Mirror	£1bn	14,000	53/£430,000
Les Hinton/21	Executive Chairman, News International; Chair of the industry's Code of Practice Committee	£16.5bn	3,800	55/£?

Tom Glocer/23	Chief Executive, Reuters	£3.59bn	18,082	41/£?
Richard Desmond/28	Chief Executive, Northern & Shell, Express Newspapers	£270m	617	48/£150m personal worth
Jonathan Harmsworth (Lord Rothermere/33	Chairman, Daily Mail & General Trust	£1.86bn	2,500	34/£415,000 (£825m personal worth)
Alistair Campbell/41	Press Secretary to PM Tony Blair	n/a	15	44/£100,000
Max Clifford/49	Founder, Max Clifford PR	?	6	58/£?
Rebekah Wade/54	Editor, *News of the World*	Circulation 3.9m	?	33/£?
Trevor Kavanagh/ 57	Political Editor, *The Sun*	Circulation 3.5m	?	?/£?
Richard Littlejohn/61	Columnist, *The Sun*	Circulation 3.5m	?	47/£?
Lord Wakeham/97	Chairman, Press Complaints Commission	n/a	n/a	69/£?

[NB figures indicated by ? were unavailable to *The Guardian*]

Some observations from the list are as follows:

- *The Sun* newspaper features highly, with three staff cited on the list.

- Rebekah Wade is the only female amongst the tabloid press cited (there were only 13 women on the top 100 in total); interestingly, she is also the youngest editor on Fleet Street.

- The preponderance of editors on this extracted list (one third) reinforces the notion that they are extremely powerful people who inevitably hold a lot of sway in terms of the content of their newspaper.

- The overwhelming majority of people on the list are middle-aged, middle-class heterosexual men who are extremely wealthy as a result of their position.

- All those with a direct relationship with the tabloid press are white.

- The emphasis is on corporate people as opposed to creative people.

Appendices

Please note that all addresses, phone and fax numbers and Web addresses were correct at the time of writing but the author and publisher can take no responsibility for the accuracy of this information in the longer term.

Useful addresses

National Union of Journalists
Acorn House
314 Grays Inn Road
London
WC1X 8DP
Tel: 020 7278 7916
Fax: 020 7837 8143

A trade union, founded in 1907, to protect and support the work of journalists.

PressWise
Easton Business Centre
Felix Road
Bristol
BS5 0HE
Tel: 0117 941 5889
Fax: 0117 941 5848

PressWise publishes helpful resources on areas such as journalists and data protection; cheque-book journalism; press inaccuracy and the Press Complaints Commission.

Campaign for Press and Broadcasting Freedom (CPBF)
8 Cynthia Street
London
N1 9JF
Tel: 020 7278 4430
Fax: 020 7837 8868

CPBF publish a variety of pamphlets, wall charts, books, videos, postcards and a bi-monthly magazine.

Press Complaints Commission (PCC)
1 Salisbury Square
London
EC4Y 8AE
Tel: 020 7353 1248 or the PCC Helpline 020 7353 3732
Fax: 020 7353 8355

PCC resolve and adjudicate over complaints about local and national newspapers and magazines.

Code of Practice Committee
c/o Press Standards Board of Finance
Merchants House Buildings
30 George Square
Glasgow
FG2 1EG

The committee deals with complaints made against the industry's Code of Practice.

Associated Newspapers Ltd
Northcliffe House
2 Derry Street
Kensington
London
W8 5TT
Tel: 020 7938 6000

The management company for *The Daily Mail, The Mail on Sunday; The Evening Standard* and *Metro* (free London paper).

The British Library
Newspaper Library
Colindale Avenue
London
NW9 5HE
Tel: 020 7412 7353
Fax: 020 7412 7379

An excellent primary source of information on the history of newspapers. They also hold copies of surviving publications.

Useful Web site addresses

- **Campaign for Press Broadcasting Freedom**
  http://www.cpbf.demon.co.uk

- **National Union of Journalists**
  http://www.gn.apc.org/media/nuj.html

- **National Readership Survey**
  http://www.nrs.co.uk

- **Press Complaints Commission**
  http://www.pcc.org.uk

- **The Guardian (media section)**
  http://www.mediaguardian.co.uk/presspublishing

- **News International**
  http://www.newsinternational.com

- **Associated Newspapers**
  http://www.associatednewspapers.co.uk

- **Daily Mail**
  http://www.dailymail.co.uk

- **The Sun**
  http://www.thesun.co.uk

- **The Daily Mirror**
  http://www.mirror.co.uk

- **News of the World**
  http://www.newsoftheworld.co.uk

- **The Daily Express**
  http://www.dailyexpress.co.uk

- **The Daily Star**
  http://www.dailystar.co.uk

- **Noam Chomsky**
  http://www.zmag.org/chomsky

- **On-line journalism review**
  http://www.ojr.usc.edu/

- **Daily newsletter and interactive site**
  http://www.journalismnet.com/uk/

- **History of journalism/press issues**
  http://www.mediahistory.com

- **Reuters news agency**
  http://www.reuters.com

- **Anorak – an e-zine which 'keeps tabs on the tabloids'**
  http://www.anorak.co.uk

- **ClariNet – on-line international news reports**
  http://www.clarinet.com

- **Site for Print Journalists**
  http://www.journalismuk.co.uk

- **British Library's History of the British Newspaper**
  http://www.bl.uk/collections/newspapers

- **Audit Bureau of Circulation**
  http://www.abc.org.uk

- **British Rates and Data**
  http://www.brad.co.uk

- **London College of Printing**
  http://www.lcp.linst.ac.uk

- **American website for Communications Studies and Media Studies teachers and students**
  http://www.cultsock.ndirect.co.uk

Bibliography and recommended reading list

Barker, H. *Newspapers and English Society 1695–1855 – Themes in British Social History Series*, Harlow, Longman: 1999.

Bell, A. *The Language of News Media*, Oxford: Blackwell, 1991.

Boyd-Barrett, O. and Braham, P. *Media, Knowledge and Power*, London: Routledge, 1990.

Branston, G. and Stafford R. *The Media Students Book*, London: Routledge, 1999.

Buckingham, D. 'The Emotional Politics of News' in *Moving Images*, Manchester, Manchester UP, 1996

Cameron, A. *Express Newspapers (The Inside Story of a Turbulent Year)*, London: London House, 2000.

Cohen, S. and Young, J. (eds) *The Manufacture of News: Deviance, Social Problems and the Mass Media*, London: Constable, 1981.

Chomsky, N. *Necessary Illusions: Thought Control in Democratic Societies*, London: Pluto Press, 1991.

Curran, J and Seaton, J. *Power Without Responsibility*, London: Routledge, 1997.

Duff, B. and Shindler, R. *Language and Style in the Press (A Reader's Guide to British Newspapers)*, Harlow: Longman, 1984.

Eldridge, J. (ed.) *Getting the Message: News, Truth and Power*, London: Routledge, 1993.

Graham, I. *Books and Newspapers – Communications Close Up*, London: Evans Brothers, 2000.

Grundy, P. *Resource Books for Teachers – Newspapers*, Oxford: OUP, 1993.

Hamilton, J.M. and Krimsky, G.A. *Hold the Press (the Inside Story on Newspapers)*, Louisiana: Louisiana State UP, 1997.

Hartley, J. *Understanding News*, London: Routledge, 1982.

Herman, E.S. and Chomsky, N. *Manufacturing Consent: The Political Economy of the Mass Media*, London: Vintage, 1995.

Keeble, R. *The Newspapers Handbook – Media Practice*, London: Routledge, 2001.

Langer, J. *Tabloid Television (Popular Journalism and the 'Other News') – Communication and Society*, London: Routledge, 1997.

Langley, A. (2001) *Heinemann Profiles: Rupert Murdoch*, Oxford: Heinemann, 2001.

Lasky, M.J. *The Language of Journalism: Newspaper Culture*, Transaction, 2000.

Livesay, T. *Babes, Booze, Orgies and Aliens (The Inside Story of Sports Newspapers)*, London: Virgin, 1998.

MacShane, D. *Using the Media*, London: Pluto Press, 1979 (out-of-print).

Marris and Thornham (eds) *Media Studies: A Reader*, New York: New York UP, 2000.

Philo, G. *Glasgow University Media Group Reader Volume 2: Communication and Society – News Industry, Economy, War and Politics*, London: Routledge, 1995.

Philo, G. (ed.) *Message Received*, Harlow: Longman, 1999.

Raymond, J. (ed.) *News, Newspapers and Society in Early Modern Britain*, London: Frank Cass, 1999.

Reah, D. *The Language of Newspapers*, London: Routledge, 1998.

Reed, D. *The Power of News: The History of Reuters*, Oxford: OUP, 1999.

Self, D. (1999) *Newspapers: Media Focus: Newspapers*, Oxford: Heinemann, 1999.

Schudson, M. *The Power of News*, New York: Harvard UP, 1996.

Shawcross, W. *Rupert Murdoch*, London: Pan, 1993.

Sloan, B. *I Watched a Wild Hog Eat My Baby: A Colourful History of Tabloids and Their Cultural Impact*, London: Prometheus, 2001.

Sova, D. (1998) *How to Write Articles for Newspapers*, Arco, 1998.

Strinati and Wagg (eds) *Come on Down? (The Politics of Popular Media Culture in Post-War Britain)*, London: Routledge, 1992.

Tunstall, J. *Newspaper Power – The New National Press in Britain*, Oxford: OUP, 1996.

Wedgbury, C. *Revolutionary Newspapers*, Killeen Books, 1998.

Williams, F. (1959) *Dangerous Estates – the Anatomy of Newspapers* (currently out of print).